The THINGS WE DO...

BY ARDYCE C. WHALEN

COPYRIGHT 2012 BY ARDYCE C. WHALEN

IN MEMORY OF EDVARD MUNCH,

WHOSE LITHOGRAPH, *THE SCREAM,*

VEHEMENTLY PORTRAYS THE HUMAN

CONDITION.

TABLE OF CONTENTS

A little about the author and the content of *The THINGS WE DO:*

I chose to write about the above topics because they greatly concern me. I am the mother of five children, with children of their own. I worry about the kind of lives they'll have. I was also a teacher of junior and senior high students while my children were growing up, and I know how confusing the teen years can be—for two months, until a birthday came along, I had five teenagers. The world back then was no picnic, but it seems more messed up now it was then. We've made great advances in areas such as medicine and technology, but in other areas we seem to have regressed, "devolved." Suicide among teens has increased 300 percent since the 1950's. Something is wrong.

WRITING WORKSHOP of Ardyce C. Whalen, ardicw@cox.net

<u>Introduction</u>

We live in trying times; so much so that it often makes one want to scream! All over the world, people fight. "My way or the highway," seems to be everyone's motto. No one wants to listen to anyone else.

Our world is not a loving place; if anything it is the opposite: a lusting place. Lust, masquerading as love, too often gets us into trouble. We hurt others, we break the law, we spread disease, we often get divorced when lust wears off, and then we break our children's hearts.

Rape is a nasty power play. One person inflicts his desire to degrade or control on another. Rape has become more common; it's even part of the rewards of war! This is evolution in reverse: the devolution of man.

Women, out of dire necessity often choose to prostitute themselves; it is their bodies and they do have that right. Women—kidnapped, sold, or lied to about nonexistent jobs—are forced to become prostitutes. This is a crime worthy of strong punishment. Men who visit them may get a sexually transmitted disease and bring it home to their wives and children. As long as there is a demand for prostitutes, there will be a supply; it is futile to try and stamp it out. The answer is regulation and protection. Make it safer for the suppliers and the demanders.

Birth is a natural process, making hospitalization unnecessary in most cases. Home births, unless complications are expected, are actually safer, and they more easily allow for the essential, skin-to-skin bonding between mother and baby, right after the birth.

It is not surprising that crime and violence are escalating, especially among our children. Our children are violent because they learn by observation, and what they observe is not pretty. We must change their view.

Schools need to do a much better job educating our children. As of now, they are truly failing our children. Single-sex classrooms have proven to be more effective in teaching both sexes than co-ed classrooms. Girls and boys learn differently, and if classrooms, or entire schools, are devoted to one sex, the teaching can be tailored appropriately. Separate can be equal and can lead to more equal opportunities.

The THINGS WE DO

We are so into technology. It follows us and clamors for our attention no matter where we are. The cell phone is our best buddy. Televisions and computers are even in our bedrooms. They're fun, but they may be the ruin of us, especially television. Television messes with our ability to imagine; if we can't imagine, we can't learn. Read it and weep.

The THINGS WE DO

Essay 1—The Things We Do for Lust

Amy Grant's song, "The Things We Do for Love," is beautiful. Too often, however, the things we think we are doing for love, we are actually doing for lust. "Love" and "lust" are opposites, but the English language has so overused the word "love," applying it to objects—"I love that sweater," or maybe, "I love my truck"—that today it is almost meaningless. For the purpose of the following argument, "love" is defined as an intense affectionate concern for another person. The poet William Blake writes of such a love in the first verse of "The Clod & the Pebble":

> Love seeketh not itself to please
> Nor for itself hath any care.
> But for another gives its ease.
> And builds a Heaven in Hell's despair.

Lust, on the other hand, is defined here as excessive or unrestrained sexual desire. Robert Burton graphically describes the seriousness of lust as follows: "Thunder and lightning, wars, fires, plagues, have not done that mischief to mankind as this burning lust, this brutish passion" (The Anatomy of Melancholy III). Though both men and women are capable of lust, men are more likely to have excessive and unrestrained sexual desire. Usually, the "object" of their lust is a woman, but it can also be another man or even a child. The world would be a far better and happier place without the mischief caused by lust.

Sex, of course, is necessary for the continuation of our species, and it is difficult to accomplish this without desire, but desire that is excessive or unrestrained, i.e., lust, presents a "clear and present danger" to society. The crux of the problem lies in the difference between the male and female sex drive, and the resultant disharmony.

Dr. Leonard Shlain writes about the trouble caused by the disparity between the sex drives in his book, Sex, Time and Power. "Whereas she was gaining control over her sex drive, his was increasing its power over him. More and more his sex urges seized control and dictated his actions. His runaway sexual agitation increased unabated until Homo sapiens became the most sex-crazed male of any living species." (109)

Testosterone makes a man a man. This hormone builds muscle, increases strength, and makes a man aggressive. He covets and respects rank and power. Testosterone makes a man willing to take risks (he can have as much as ten times the amount of testosterone as a woman). "This hormone weakens the bonds of love and attachment." A testosterone-fueled man, and they all are to some degree, seeks to dominate and control those he considers weaker or more cautious than he is (Shlain, 343). His strength, aggressiveness, and willingness to take risks have made him Earth's most successful predator.

In the early days of Homo sapiens, the bravest hunters got the most sex. Women needed the iron in red meat to compensate for blood loss during menstruation and childbirth, so the hunter that could supply the meat, got a "YES![1] Men soon learned to associate hunting success with sex (Shlain, 108-14). With the advent of agriculture, men could raise their own livestock. They didn't have to hunt wild game to get the red meat that would get them sex. Yet hunting had been exciting and rewarding, and it had led to exciting and rewarding sex. Man, still the hunter, just changed what he hunted: the sex "object" now became the prey (on occasion, out of need or for recreation, men still hunted animals). The chorus of Stuart Hamblen's song, "I Won't Go Huntin' with You Jake," says it all:

> Oh, I won't go huntin' with you, Jake, but I'll go chasin' women

So put them hounds back in the pens and quit your silly
grinnin'

Well, the moon is bright, and I'm half tight; my life is just
beginnin'

I won't go huntin' with you, Jake, but I'll go chasin'
women.

It is not an accident that some men refer to a woman's breasts as a "rack," the same slang word used for a deer's antlers.

Before we start to "Dream the Impossible Dream," the achievement of a lust-free world, let's see just how destructive lust can be. First, we'll look at a couple of familiar instances from the past, and then we'll look at the damage lust does in society today.

Mythology tells the story of Helen of Troy and the Trojan prince, Paris. Paris had to choose the most beautiful goddess from among three (Hera, Athena, and Aphrodite), and he chose Aphrodite because she had promised to give him the world's most beautiful woman, Helen of Troy.

Paris soon sailed to Greece and was welcomed hospitably by Menelaus, Helen's husband, with whom she was living happily. Aphrodite, however, put her under a spell that caused Helen to elope with Paris, who then carried her off to Troy. Menelaus called upon the Greek chieftains to help him rescue Helen. Most responded to his call, and thus began the ten-year Trojan War ("Helen").

The Bible contains many examples of the troubles caused by lust. Among the most familiar is the story of King David and Bathsheba. King David was so smitten by the sight of Bathsheba at her bath, that he seduced her while her soldier husband, Uriah, was away. She became pregnant. When David could not persuade her husband that the child was Uriah's and not his, he arranged to have Uriah killed in battle (2 Samuel, 11:2-26).

A man will risk a war and another will have a rival killed all because they could not control their excessive desires. Ah, the power of lust! It plays a major role in the escalating divorce rate around the world. Helen E. Fisher, writing in Psychology Today, lists overt adultery as the main cause of divorce, followed by sterility and barrenness. (Third place on her list is cruelty, particularly by a husband towards his wife.) Other reasons for the increase in the divorce rate, particularly in industrialized countries, is the decrease in a couple's economic need for each other, and an increase in the improvement of birth control methods, allowing people to separate sex from reproduction ("Quick Answers").

Separating sex from reproduction allows it to become a game for the curious. They forget the old saying, "curiosity killed the cat." Robert S. Boyd wrote in article appearing in the Arizona Daily Star of November 16, 2003, "Mate Poachers, Poachees Rife in Romance's Jungle." The article deals with behaviors in "love" triangles, the two most common being "mate poaching," an attempt to steal someone else's mate; and "mate guarding," a strategy used to thwart the would-be thief. According to David Buss, a University of Texas professor, a survey of 1,242 Midwesterners aged twenty to sixty-five found that nearly half "had managed to steal—or borrow—someone else's wife, husband, girlfriend or boyfriend."

Another study by Buss and his associate, David Schmitt, reports that 60 percent of men and 30 percent of women "sought out brief sexual flings with other people's mates on one or more occasions." Schmitt reports nearly a 50 percent success rate (Boyd). These people are playing a game that is usually fatal to real love; they are "hunters" on the loose, trying to poach "game" to which they have no right. For a little selfish, lusty fun, they are breaking hearts and breaking up families.

Teenagers and Sex

If strong feelings of desire are difficult for adults to control, it is much harder for young people who are on an emotional roller coaster most of the time. Teenage boys think almost constantly about sex. Shlain describes their situation as follows: "A postpubescent boy's sexual desires nearly drive him mad as his brain soaks in a cranial tub laced with testosterone" (139). In the United States, "two out of three boys have had sex by age eighteen" ("General Facts"). At the onset of puberty, "testosterone floods the young male's incompletely myelinated[2] brain, creating a dangerous and unstable situation" (Shlain, 344). Teens tend to act on impulse, not taking the time to reason, as they would do if their brains were fully mature.

The United States is the leader of the Western industrialized world when it comes to the number of teen pregnancies and births. The bill for this situation is a whopping nine billion dollars ($9,000,000,000!) each year ("11 Facts about Teen Pregnancy"). Yet, in spite of these figures, the United States has trouble providing much needed education to young people about how to take care of their bodies, including sex education, because of the complaints of a few.

Even with the improvements in birth control, nearly eighty-two percent of the 750,000 teen pregnancies occurring on average each year, are unplanned (Guttmacher Institute's "Fact Sheet").

This coupling of lust and ignorance is a national disgrace. The younger the pregnant girl, the more likely was she to have been a victim of lust. "Close to four in ten girls who had first intercourse at 13 or 14 report it was either non-voluntary or unwanted." In fact, "three out of four girls and over half of boys report that girls who have sex do so because their boyfriends want them to" (quoted in "General Facts"). Psychiatrist John Bancroft, M.D., Director of the Kinsey Institute, declares, "The United States is a mess, as far as sex is concerned" (quoted by Mendelsohn).

Perhaps to put some common sense into the way we deal with sex, President Bill Clinton made Jocelyn Elders Surgeon General of the United States. She advocated sex education to avoid unwanted pregnancy. She also thought that young people should have free access to condoms, and that boys should practice getting them on right by masturbating in them. "It's way more educational and fun than putting one on a banana" (quoted in "Too Honest"). The article goes on to say: "Apparently, the moral majority is perfectly happy with a country full of stupid pregnant kids." Jocelyn Elders was pressured to resign. The pregnant kids may be uneducated and lustful, but they are not the stupid ones.

Child Sexual Abuse

Girls are not the only victims, or "prey," of the lustful, boys are often victims too. Child pornography—boys and girls---is illegal in the United States, but those who want it have only to sit down at their computers. A report, authored by John Carr, shows that child porn crimes have increased by one thousand five hundred percent (1,500%) since 1988. He told the BBC Radio Five Live: "In pre-Internet days, if you wanted to get hold of child abuse images it was quite a difficult thing to do ....The Internet completely changed all that. People, perhaps with a suppressed or latent interest in it, have now got a mechanism ... they think the Internet is anonymous." Lest people in the United States feel morally superior over these statistics from Britain, "In 2002, in a single day 6,500 Britons were identified as purchasers of child porn from a *single* US web site [italics added]" ("Net Blamed").

The anonymity of the Internet makes it a favorite place for the lustful to go for sexually explicit images, but places exist where one would never expect to find lustful predators. Churches have traditionally been places of sanctuary, places where moral values are taught. This is not the case in too many Catholic parishes where victims have accused priests of gross immorality. Vows of celibacy are broken as these "Fathers" sexually abuse and rape children, particularly boys. A survey of Catholic dioceses in the United States for the Washington Post, reports: "The Roman Catholic church removed 218 priests from their positions in 2002, because of allegations of child sexual abuse, but at least 34 known offenders remain in church jobs." The same survey found that of the 850 U.S. priests accused of sexual abuse of minors since the 1960's, more than 350 of them had been removed from the ministry prior to 2002. Many survey responders, diocesan spokesmen, stated that they didn't know the sex or exact ages of the children being molested (Cooperman and Sun). The victims know, and they also know that trust has died.

Child sexual abuse is not confined to images on the Internet and to lustful clergy. Reverend Ron Rolheiser, OMI (Oblates of Mary Immaculate), puts the church sexual abuse crisis into context when he states:

> It's estimated that, in the Western world, one out of every four or five persons, girls and boys, comes to adulthood scarred, having been violated sexually in either a major way or minor way, though it's rare the violation is minor because by nature all sexual abuse is serious. In terms of an image, this means that [statistically] some form of sexual abuse is happening in every fourth or fifth house in the Western world.

Reverend Rolheiser is correct when he adds the home as a place where sexual abuse occurs, but he left out the field of athletics, as proved by the recent scandal at Penn State. Jerry Sandusky, former Pennsylvania State University assistant football coach, was indicted on fifty-two counts of child molestation from the years 1994 to 2009, though the abuse may go back as far as the 1970's (Wikipedia). No matter what form or where the abuse takes place, the molestation of children is a betrayal of innocence and trust. Children are our leaders of tomorrow; what kind of leaders will they be if their childhood has been sabotaged?

Pornography

In the United States, child pornography is illegal, but adult pornography is not. Advertisers have long known that males are wired to respond to visual stimulation. Females tend to respond more to sounds. Some of you, me included, may remember all those teen-aged girls swooning when Frank Sinatra sang. And do you remember the stories about all those rock-n-roll groupies? Today young girls and the paparazzo are chasing Justin Bieber. The turn-on afforded by magazines such as Playboy, pales in comparison to the loads of sexual images available in television, films, and Internet sites.[3] Adult porn is pervasive, available twenty-four hours a day, seven days a week, and you can even get it on your cell phone! Though few makers of pornography show their actors practicing safe sex, Vivid Entertainment, noted for their porn flicks, uses condoms in all its films, believing it to be the "socially responsible" thing to do (Kisken).

According to 60 Minutes, November 23, 2003, pornography has become popular, "cool," and part of the teenage rebellion. A poll taken by the Kaiser Family Foundation in 2001, reports that "70 percent of teenagers accidentally come across pornography online." The polltakers interviewed teens in the fifteen to twenty-four-year old age bracket. Of those teens, "59 percent [said] they believe seeing porn on the Internet encourages young people to have sex before they are ready; 49 percent said it promotes bad attitudes toward women and encourages viewers to think unprotected sex is O.K." (Paul, 101).

Mark Schwartz, director of the Masters and Johnson clinic in St. Louis, fears that men will come to view women as just a collection of parts, and that they will come to depend on visual imagery for arousal. He says, "The image of a lonely, isolated man masturbating to his computer is the Willy Loman metaphor of our decade." Experts fear that men, with such unrealistic attitudes toward women, their appearance and behavior, may find it very difficult to form a lasting relationship with women in ordinary, day to day, life. Ordinary women may fail to sexually satisfy (Paul, 99).

Addiction to cybersex, online porn, disrupts the lives of 15 percent of habitual watchers, according to Alvin Cooper, who conducts seminars on this form of "sexual compulsiveness" (Paul, 99). The industry doesn't care; they are raking in the money. Pornography is now the number one corporate entity, earning about ten billion dollars a year ("Porn in the US"). That's a lot of money spent to fan the flames of lust; it's akin to pouring gasoline on a fire.

Flames, "cleansing fires," have been used to halt the spread of disease during epidemics, but these burning flames have the opposite effect; they spread disease. In 2002 there were over 1,200,000 reported cases of sexually transmitted diseases (STDs) in the United States ("Table 2"). Statistics for the United Kingdom in the year 2003 show that "708,083 people in England, Wales and Northern Ireland were diagnosed with an STI [Sexually Transmitted Infection] in 2003." Interestingly, the article containing the statistics about STI in the United Kingdom, blames most of the infections on the behavior of a "promiscuous 10 percent" of the population. The people making up this 10 percent experienced sex "at an early stage and have multiple partners," according to professor Mark Bellis and his colleagues of the John Moores University research team in Liverpool. ("Promiscuous 10%")

Great strides have been made in the treatment of HIV/AIDS, but it remains a serious, worldwide problem. As of July 2012, over thirty-four million people worldwide live with HIV/AIDS, 3.4 million are children under the age of fifteen ("Statistics: Worldwide").

We know that AIDS is out of control in Africa, but some believe that India is the most AIDS infected country in the world. If it is not contained soon, it could severely weaken India's army and her economy. The economy of the United States would then be affected; indeed, the United States could also be infected with a new AIDS epidemic, reports Correspondent Bob Simon. He is not the only one who is concerned, Colin Powell told the United Nations more than a year after 9/11: "AIDS is more devastating than any terrorist attack, any conflict, or any weapon of mass destruction. AIDS can destroy countries and destabilize entire regions" (Rebecca Leung).

India's prostitutes have been hit the hardest by the AIDS epidemic. About 20 percent of their customers are truckers, and many have little idea of how AIDS is spread. Some believe that just bathing after having sex with a prostitute will take care of the problem. The few prostitutes who would discuss AIDS, say that condoms are "bad for business," so along with their assigned deliveries, these truckers deliver AIDS all across India and to their own wives as well. Dr. Suniti, who first detected AIDS among prostitutes over ten years ago, now carries a patient load that is 90 percent monogamous women who contracted HIV from their husbands (Leung). Ignorance combined with lust makes for a deadly concoction.

Forced Prostitution

Forced prostitution is slavery. All over the world, writes Jennifer Schroeder, women and children are forced into prostitution to satisfy human lust. Most of the people trafficked in the United States are for the sex trade, for repayment of a debt, or for labor, such as domestic, dancing, or agriculture. United States citizens, who are trafficked, almost always end up in the sex industry. Children that run away from home or who are homeless are prime victims ("Human Trafficking in the United States"). Grigoris Lazos, a sociology professor, researched prostitution in Greece in 1999. He talked to the prostitutes themselves, and eventually he was able to contact their enslavers. He found that there is a big difference between a small trafficking group and a large network. With the small group, he says:

Any bar owner or group of bar owners in Greece can send someone up to southern Bulgaria to buy women for cash. The cost of a girl in that area is $1,000, or, if you negotiate, you might be able to get two for $1,000. Best to try on a Monday for cheap prices. Mondays are slow, so you can get leftovers. (quoted in Cockburn).

A large network uses bank accounts and the Internet, and can complete transactions from a distance. Grigoris explained: "Simply call Moscow, ask for women, and they will be sent to Romania and from there on to Bulgaria to Greece. The parties don't even have to know each other" (quoted in Cockburn). What goes on with forced prostitution in Greece is not at all unique, states Cockburn.

Child prostitution is a scourge in many countries, including Thailand, where efforts are being made to eradicate it. Thailand's Crime Suppression Division commander blames the child prostitution problem on foreigners. In particular, he addresses the problem of boy prostitutes: "There are quite a few places where boys are provided for sexually demented foreigners including entertainment places ....There are also agents who contact customers at various hotels to offer boys under their control to customers for sex ....In order to suppress child prostitution we are trying to cut the links between suppliers and customers, as well as monitoring the activities of foreigners with strange sexual urges and desires" (quoted in Jirapinyo).

The Fury of a Man Scorned

Child prostitution is an abomination. Could anything be worse? There may be. In certain countries, when a man in "lust" is rejected, he may throw acid at the one who rejected him. He may act out of passion, but the passion is not love, because love is "an intense affectionate concern for another person." Only revenge and despicable selfishness drive these men to acid-attack their victims, leaving serious physical and emotional scars.

In Bangladesh, so many women have been disfigured by acid attacks, reports Manoshi Barua, that they have formed Acid Survivors Foundation in Dhaka, the capital, to help women deal with the trauma. Their disfigurement came about because they rejected the advances of men. One woman tells her story:

> She had two sons and she engaged a private tutor for them. Then he started to make some advances. She kept asking him to stop but he continued. Then she told the tutor that she had told her husband about his advances. One evening ... the tutor poured acid over her body, which damaged her skull. It made her blind in one eye; she became partially sighted with the other eye. Her whole face, chest, wrist and hand got burned (Barua).

25

Bangladesh is not the only place where such brutal acts of revenge occur. India has her share of them, and again, spurned lust causes men to behave in a particularly vicious and cowardly way, with absolutely no concern for their victims. Acid attacks do not kill the body, but they can kill the spirit over and over again. Gautam Singh describes such an attack in an article titled, "Acid Attacks Take Brutal Toll in India":

> She's blind and disfigured. Her college friends don't visit anymore, and children are terrified of her. On rare trips out of the house, she hides behind a cotton scarf. Her anger still burns. Five years ago, Haseena Huyssein's former boss flung acid onto her, angry that the woman he'd become infatuated with resisted coming back to work for him.

In early May her attacker, Joseph Rodrigues, was sentenced to five years and three months in jail, and ordered to pay her $6,666. Her care and skin grafts have cost her family $15,555 so far. "Even if I die," says Haseena, "I'll never forgive him" (Singh). Haseena Huyssein no longer lives; she merely exists in a world where the future is devoid of hope and filled with pain and hatred.

Over thirty cases of acid attacks in the past five years have been documented in Karnataka state, India (Singh).

Rape

An essay on lust would not be complete without writing about rape. Though always violent, rape is more frequently about control or revenge rather than lust. However, in South Africa, rape is the order of the day, and those who rape don't think they've done anything wrong. According to Dempster, "A woman born in South Africa has a greater chance of being raped than learning how to read." Men believe that they are sexually entitled to women, and the women believe it too; they don't say no to a man (Dempster).

Childline, a child support group, reports that 25 percent of girls in South Africa are raped before the age of sixteen. Even babies are raped. Over the past decade, sexual violence against children has increased 400 percent, according to a report presented at a recent parliamentary debate. Most horrendous, is that "many of the perpetrators are themselves children" (Dempster). Seemingly, women and children are merely depositories for men's semen, and like a tissue or paper towel, discarded after use. With such cultural attitudes, what does the future hold for this country?

Possible Solutions

These, then, are some of the wages of lust. The cost in human suffering and pain is incalculable and heart-rending. To just delineate a problem without offering any hope of solution would be pointless. Therefore, we will now examine some possible solutions that will at least help to lessen the number of lust's victims.

Thoughtful people, joining together, can change the world and make it a safer and happier place for all, especially for women and children. We can educate, pass necessary laws, and enforce those that exist. We can join and support organizations fighting to right the wrongs perpetrated by lust. Most importantly, individuals can employ sexual selection in such a way that the lustful, those who lack self-control, do not reproduce.

Lust has no right to sadden and disrupt the life of a child. A child needs love, yes, but not lust; if you've forgotten the difference, go back and read the start of this essay. A child also needs a secure family, ideally with a mother and a father, but there are other satisfactory arrangements—the most important ingredient is unselfish love for the child. A high divorce rate, with infidelity the main cause given for divorce, endangers family security. Our children are the future: Don't mess with the future. Refuse to let lust tear families apart. A couple of strategies, one practical, the other verging on science fiction, could drastically reduce the divorce rate.

Opting for practicality, a couple "in love" would enter into a formal "trial cohabitation," lasting three years. According to Tennov and Money, if their "love" was actually lust, by the end of three years the passion would be gone (quoted by Fisher, "Biology"). They could then simply go their separate ways. If, however, their strong feelings for each other were actually the beginning of love, or had turned into mutual love, the couple could then enter into a real marriage and have children if they chose.

The science fiction strategy explained below, is not yet available, but when it is, it will practically guarantee marital fidelity.

First, some background: Meadow voles and prairie voles are cousins. Meadow voles are promiscuous, while prairie voles are faithful. Scientists know that a hormone called "vasopressin" accounts for the pair bonding of prairie voles; they also know that the promiscuous meadow voles have fewer vasopressin receptors in their brains. When researchers gave the meadow voles extra vasopressin receptors, they became attentive and "home loving," mating only with one female even when tempted by other females. Vasopressin is released when humans have sex. It is believed to produce a reward, a "good" feeling, abetting the bond between the partners (Kettlewell).

Scientists will keep working on this, and perhaps someday a spouse who has a "roving eye" may be happily domesticated by a dose of vasopressin receptor gene.

Teen Pregnancy

With the advances in birth control methods, it is shameful that close to half of the teenage pregnancies in the United States are unintended. This most definitely calls for education. . Teens need to know about the seriousness and prevalence of sexually transmitted diseases and how best to take care for their bodies, and this includes birth control information. Though abstinence is the ideal, not all can, or will, refrain from "doing it"; they need to know about contraceptive methods. No country wants to have uneducated, pregnant kids.

Single-sex education may be part of the solution: "Teenage sex and unwanted teenage pregnancy are much more common at coed schools than at single-sex schools." In coed schools, a girl's boyfriend is part of her circle of friends, her social life. If having sex is what the group does, it's hard for a girl to say no. Breaking up puts her entire social life in jeopardy. That is not the case in a single-sex school because a girl's circle of friends will probably not be the same as her boyfriend's; therefore, it's easier for her to say no. Saying no will not destroy her social network. She has more autonomy, more control; she can live without the boyfriend if she has to ("Advantages for Girls").[4]

Teen boys who are "fizzing" with testosterone can take themselves "in hand." The myth about "hairy palms" as a result is NOT TRUE. Above all, however, boys need appropriate adult males to teach them self-discipline. Boys should not be forcing girls into having a sexual relationship.

We can take a lesson from the animal kingdom. In an African park, adult elephants were separated from orphaned youngsters. When these youngsters began to mature, the "boys" ganged together and became extremely aggressive. They raped and killed endangered white rhinos. What to do? Ten adult bulls were brought in to "straighten out" these young delinquents, these ruffians. It worked. Life became normal, and elephant and rhino lived in peace (Lower).

Teenaged boys so very much need good fathers to guide them.

HIV/AIDS—A Huge Problem

HIV/AIDS is still a very serious and worldwide problem. Misinformation makes a bad situation far worse. The misinformed fathers in India who bring HIV/AIDS home to their wives because they think just bathing after a visit to an infected prostitute will be enough to prevent infection, desperately need correct information and guidance. So do the men in Africa who believe that having sex with a virgin will cure AIDS. Blanketing the world with solid, true information is the only way to dispel the myths and mistaken ideas about this terrible disease.

In Kenya, Africa, where HIV/AIDS has been declared a national disaster, there is a program using a mobile phone text message service to get out correct information. Subscribers get daily tips on prevention of HIV/AIDS in this country where "more 1.5 million people [have] died" from AIDS. This is a practical way to spread information because 2.5 million Kenyans have a mobile phone (five times more than those with internet access), and the number of people owning cell phones will grow. Text questions are sent in, the database is researched, and a response is sent back to the person's mobile phone. The non-governmental organization, One World, launched the service on 01 December 2004, World Aids Day ("Texts Aim").

HIV/AIDS infects the prostitutes of India and of other places. Often their clients refuse to wear condoms because it reduces their pleasure. Not only do these sex workers need education about HIV/AIDS, but also they need to have their work legalized so that they can be protected under the law. Furthermore, they need a union. With strength in numbers, they can demand safeguards, such as condom use and health care. By safeguarding their health, the lives of countless wives and children may be saved, since men will then be far less likely to bring home sexually transmitted diseases.

According to statistics, "An estimated 34 million people are living with the virus, down from 38.1 million in 2003." Over the years, however, it is the women of the world who are becoming infected with HIV in ever increasing numbers. "The steepest increases among women occurred in East Asia (56 percent), followed by Eastern Europe (48 percent) and Central Asia (48 percent). "[In] Africa ... women account for nearly 60 percent of infected people" ("HIV in Women").

Dr. Peter Piot, director of the U.N. AIDS program in Geneva, said that worldwide prevention and treatment programs must focus on women to stop the epidemic. "Male-to-female HIV transmission during sex is twice as likely to occur as female-to male transmission." Layers of cervical cells make women more susceptible to infection. As things stand now, compared with men, "A disproportionately small number of women are receiving anti-HIV drugs." They cost too much; they can't afford them (quoted in "HIV in Women").

When a woman's husband dies, in the majority of places in this world, it is customary that the widow is left with nothing, she is poverty-stricken. Her only option, if she wants to live, is to sell her body. Legal action is needed to protect women from violence (even within marriage), and to give them inheritance rights. Women, and girls, need basic education and opportunities for employment, so that, if necessary, they can support themselves ("HIV in Women"). Prostitution should not be their only alternative to starvation. "There was reason enough before AIDS, but now the link between the whole gender inequality and death has never been so direct as with AIDS. If AIDS is not enough to shift the agenda for women, then what is enough?" (Piot quoted in "U.N: Women's Rights Crucial").

The fear of death about 150,000 years ago gave woman the strength to say no to man because she feared dying in childbirth (Shlain, 5-7; 19-21). Let's hope that she can again summon such strength of will and say no to the man who won't wear a condom, and no to the man that in any way harms her. This time it will be harder, because our patriarchal world has stripped women of their support system, their sisters. To support them they have only the law, which too often rules in favor of men or is not enforced. Perhaps, as in the distant past, if enough women die, those that are left will regain the power to say, "No!"

Pornography, Pedophilia, and Forced Prostitution

Adults can legally make and view pornography. Article 19 of the "Universal Declaration of Human Rights" reads as follows: "Everyone has the right to freedom of opinion and expression; this right includes freedom to hold opinions without interference and to seek, receive and impart information and ideas through any media and regardless of frontiers" (4).

If adults become addicted to pornography to the extent that it interferes with their normal life, they can seek help. Again, it's their choice. When it comes to children, however, it's another matter.

The Convention on the Rights of the Child was adopted internationally fifteen years ago (1989). Article 34 is as follows:

> States Parties undertake to protect the child from all forms of sexual abuse. For these purposes, States Parties shall in particular take all appropriate national, bilateral and multilateral measures to prevent:

(a) The inducement to coercion of a child to engage in any unlawful sexual activity

(b) The exploitative use of children in prostitution or other unlawful sexual practices

(c)The exploitative use of children in pornographic performances and materials

Since its adoption, every country in the world has ratified it except two, the United States and Somalia ("Convention on the Rights"). More than half of the countries have made it a part of their state law, and nearly a third entered its important precepts into their constitutions. The document has led to the establishment of "more than sixty independent human rights institutions for children in at least thirty-eight states around the world" (quoted in "Despite Progress").

Adoption and ratification are only a first step. Elimination of child pornography and prostitution cry out for enforcement of these principles. They must be made a part of a country's legal system, and then strictly enforced. Child pornography is a worldwide scourge, stamping it out will require worldwide cooperation, commitment, and resources.

In 1991 an organization was established in Bangkok for just such a purpose, End Child Prostitution in Asian Tourism (ECPAT). It now consists of 250 groups, forming the ECPAT network, which operates in over twenty-five countries. Its mission statement is as follows:

> ECPAT is a global network of organizations and individuals working together for the elimination of child prostitution, child pornography and the trafficking of children for sexual purposes. It seeks to encourage the world community to ensure that children everywhere enjoy their fundamental rights free and secure from all forms of commercial sexual exploitation. (Akdeniz)

People concerned about the sexual exploitation of children are encouraged to join and support such organizations.

A closely related area to child prostitution and child pornography is hidden child sexual abuse, or pedophilia. A new worldwide website has been launched on which the suspicious actions of possible sexual abusers can be reported. Neil Bennett, crime correspondent for the BBC, says the website, called Virtual Global Task Force (VGTF), is run by "international law enforcement agencies." Police officers will be able to use the website to gather evidence. Microsoft and AOL will have a link on their websites to the VGTF. The VGTF is comprised of the National Crime Squad (NCS) in the United Kingdom, the Royal Canadian Mounted Police, Australia's Hi-Tech Crime Centre, the United States Department of Security and Interpol.

Deputy Director General of the NCS, Jim Gamble, wants to get the message out that they are the "sheriff" of the World Wide Web, and that it is not a safe place for pedophiles to operate (quoted in Bennett).

Exploiters of children deserve all the punishment the law allows. If such incidents occur within a church, a place where people supposedly find refuge, they are particularly egregious. In spite of recent ubiquitous newspaper headlines, pedophilia is not only a problem for religious organizations. Reverend Ron Rolheiser, OMI, says, "Less than .01 percent of this massive problem" can be blamed on priests. "Pedophilia" he states, "is not a celibate or gay disease … It plays no favorites. It's a sickness … caused by some massive trauma in childhood" (Rolheiser). This massive trauma may itself be child abuse, and the beat goes on.

An article in Psychology Today, "The Mind of a Child Molester," gives us a look inside a traumatized mind that became sick. "Alan X." became a child molester after his mother caught him masturbating. She, who was usually cold and unemotional, freaked out, and dragged him into the bathroom to scrub him clean. From that day on his mother was his enemy, and he became obsessed with thoughts of molestation. Before he was caught, "this cunning sociopath manipulated and molested more than 1,000 boys by becoming their best friend." He pleaded guilty and was given multiple life sentences with no parole (X. with Hammel-Zabin). A victim himself, he managed to leave behind so many more victims. If Rolheiser is correct about pedophilia's cause, having and enforcing laws against it aren't enough; we need to rethink our child raising methods.

Both children and adults suffer sexual abuse in the form of forced prostitution, which is actually slavery--a slavery that is banned in most of the countries where it is practiced, and a slavery that almost everyone in the world agrees is wrong. Women and children are sold like objects, forced to provide sex, and are at the mercy of their "employers."

The United Nations General Assembly adopted and proclaimed a "Universal Declaration of Human Rights" in 1948; Article 4 reads: "No one shall be held in slavery or servitude; slavery and the slave trade shall be prohibited in all their forms." Any country not yet banning slavery should do so immediately. Below are three things that must happen to end slavery:

> 1) Public awareness has to grow, and there has to be public agreement that it is time to end slavery once and for all. This public commitment must be communicated to politicians.

> 2) Money needs to be spent to eradicate slavery, but not nearly as much as you might think. For the price of a

bomber or a battleship, the amount of slavery in the world could be dramatically reduced.

3) Governments must enforce their own anti-slavery laws. To make this happen every country has to understand that they must take action or face serious pressure. We all know about the United Nations weapons inspectors, who enforce the Conventions against Weapons of Mass Destruction, but where are the United Nations slavery inspectors? When the same effort is put behind searching out and ending slavery, there will be rapid change (Bales).

Slaves outnumber masters. If we all stand with the slaves, their masters will be unable to keep them. Powerful criminals control much of the trafficking, but "slavery will end if corruption is tackled, victims are treated with respect, and those of us who are free decide to support all those who help others to freedom" (Bales).

The particular kind of prostitution that is actually slavery, calls for an additional remedy: legalization. Legalize this prostitution/slavery so that it can be regulated, and the enormous profits taken out of the business, making it of no interest to crime syndicates. Regulate it so that desperate women, women without any other marketable skills, will have a way to make a living. They deserve protection of the law rather than persecution. Lustful men could go to them instead of preying on the unwilling. The pay the prostitutes earned would be a single instance of good coming from lust. The demand will always be there, and where there is a demand, there will be a supply. For those cringing at the thought of legalizing prostitution, consider this: the Netherlands, where prostitution has never been illegal, has the least number of murders and rapes, and HIV/AIDS is not an epidemic there.

A woman's body belongs to her. Any adult woman who chooses to sell her body should have the right to do so. According to Article 23 of the "Universal Declaration of Human Rights," the right to work is everyone's right, as is protection from unemployment. In addition, everyone has a right to choose his/her line of work and to do this work in a fair and favorable environment.

"Everyone" means every adult. The "Convention on the Rights of the Child," Article 34, condemns child prostitution, as should everyone. Anyone forcing a child to be a prostitute deserves severe punishment.

As for those acid throwers seeking revenge for rejection of their advances, they deserve the same punishment they would get under their country's law if they had so criminally assaulted a man. Again, from Article 3 of the "Universal Declaration of Human Rights": "Everyone has the right to life, liberty and security of person. "Also, Article 5 (same document), "No one shall be subjected to torture or to cruel, inhuman or degrading treatment or punishment."

Would it be degrading to quarantine the "promiscuous 10 percent" who are spreading sexually transmitted infections willy-nilly with seemingly not a care in the world? If there's a "promiscuous 10 percent" in the United Kingdom, chances are there are promiscuous 10 "percenters" in other countries. The BBC News (online) reports that the promiscuous 10 percent are "fueling a UK sexual health crisis." John Moores University researchers blame poor sex education and sex on TV. The researchers conclude: "Perhaps a greater level of statutory, pertinent and timely sex education is now required despite the complaints of a few." Further, if this 10 percent cannot be persuaded to change their ways, "attempts to cut sexually transmitted infections will fail" ("Promiscuous 10%").

That's where the quarantine idea comes to the fore. If these promiscuous ones cannot be persuaded to change, they should be treated as Typhoid Mary was when she spread a communicable disease.[5] Put them under quarantine for as long as it takes for them to quit being a menace to society. Maybe they'll become addicted to cyber-sex and will no longer be satisfied with real people. We can but hope.

Finally, the whole problem of lust could be solved in a couple of generations if women had complete control of their bodies; in particular, of their uteruses. Men who could not control their lust, would not be allowed to plant their seed in this most precious of organs. Robert Wright has this to say about female reproduction:

> Giving birth involves a huge commitment of time and energy, and nature has put a low ceiling on how many such enterprises she can undertake. So each child, from her (genetic) point of view, is an extremely precious gene machine. Its ability to survive is of mammoth importance.... She should size up an aspiring partner before letting him in on the investment, asking herself what he'll bring to the project.

He should not bring an out-of-control, lustful nature. Man risked his life to bring bloody meat to an iron-starved woman so that she'd give him sex. In so doing, he became the aggressive hunter woman wanted. Woman must again shape the world by her sexual selection.

If done once, it can be done again. Men want sex, and men want children, little replicas of themselves to live on after they're dead. Now women can sexually select for committed men, men who will be good fathers to their children, men who will be devoted. Marie Curie, two-time Nobel Prize winner (science), believed, "You cannot build a better society without improving individuals" (Goldsmith).

Women need to be on their guard. A study found that "males, markedly more than females, report depicting themselves as more kind, sincere, and trustworthy than they actually are" (Wright).

So-called "human nature" can be changed. To quote Robert Wright again:

> First, to say something is a product of natural selection is not to say that it is unchangeable. Just about any manifestation of human nature can be changed, given an apt alteration of the environment
>
> Second, to say that something is "natural" is not to say that it is good. Nature isn't a moral authority, and we needn't adopt any "values" that seem implicit in its workings—natural selection's indifference to the suffering of the weak, for example, is not something we need emulate.

The environment that must be changed is the environment in which many women live. Morgan, in The Descent of Woman, writes, "The first of all things women need to be liberated from is their classic tendency to feelings (admitted, concealed, or aggressively overcompensated for) of guilt and inadequacy" (240). As it reads in Article 7 of the "Universal Declaration of Human Rights":

> All are equal before the law and are entitled without any discrimination to equal protection of the law. All are entitled to equal protection against any discrimination in violation of this Declaration and against any incitement to such discrimination.

Women need to achieve economic independence (this will bring with it a great deal of respect), and have rights of inheritance and the right to own property. If women choose to marry, they must choose whom they will marry. Only those women who want children need have them, and only as many as they want. These things must come to pass in order to again give women the power to say, "No!" (Morgan, 242-250). Humanity will benefit when all woman can say, "No!"

Conclusion

The world can be changed for the better; it can be happier and safer. Right now we live in a world where lust is breaking apart marriages, children are having children, and TV is the cheerleader. Pornography is very big business, and getting bigger. It's available twenty-four hours a day. Though illegal in many countries, child pornography is not difficult to find on the Internet, and now it can even be found on cell phones. Many men consider women inferior objects, of use mostly for reproductive and recreational sex. Women are often forced into prostitution, and so are children—the most despicable form of slavery. Our lust-crazed world is rife with sexually transmitted diseases. This "brutish passion" makes its victims' life a Hell.

We need not be helpless victims. We can conquer lust if those possessing self-control all work together. Our families need strengthening; the importance of a stable marriage with loving, cooperating parents cannot be overemphasized. It's time to take our heads out of the sand and recognize the needs of our young people for sex education that includes contraception if they will not abstain.

Many countries have laws, good laws, against child pornography and prostitution, but they need to be strictly enforced, or what good are they? Concerning prostitution, it's common sense to legalize it. Doing so would provide a needed outlet for those that are either sex-starved or sex-crazed. If it is legalized, it can be regulated and made safer and healthier. Legalizing prostitution would cut trafficking profits for crime syndicates, and it would also cut down on other crimes, such as rape and murder.

Lastly, a woman can be part of the ultimate solution by taking heed of whose sperm starts a baby growing within her uterus, and it is hers, it's in her body. She needs to sexually select for quality: no lustful, out-of-control man should reproduce. In two generations, our world would be happier and safer.

This essay gave two examples of damaging, historical lust—the abduction of Helen of Troy and the seduction of Bathsheba. Now it ends with a historical example of love. The Mughal emperor of the 1600s, Shah Jehan, built the Taj Mahal and the elaborate formal gardens surrounding it in Āgra, to honor his wife. When Mumtaz, his wife and the mother of his children, died in 1630, the Shah was grief-stricken. He built the Taj Mahal as a way of keeping her memory alive (Crown).

The THINGS WE DO

Essay 2— Rape: The Devolution of Man

DESPOLIATION

He sang as he brutally raped;

No matter that she was but eight.

DESECRATION

Blood on his rod

Cries out to God,

"Please STOP this

Pogrom of HATE!"

ABOMINATION

D E V O L U T I O N[6]

The cartoon image of a cave man clubbing a woman on the head and dragging her off into the bushes is neither amusing nor exaggerated. Rape has been with us for a very long time. Men raped and still do rape, for a variety of reasons. Some men rape to feel powerful; others, perhaps low status males, rape because they feel it is their only chance to reproduce. In wartime, men rape to hurt the enemy by violating the enemy's "property." By law, women were property in many ancient civilizations, and to this day they still are considered so in some cultures. Fighting men may also be encouraged, or even ordered, to rape as a means of demoralizing the enemy. Then too, rape has historically been thought to be one of war's rewards, or "spoils."

Men rape in times of war, and they rape in times of peace. Rape, however, has now devolved from an act often expected during wartime or an act of random aggression, into an increasingly cold, calculated, and vicious crime against human rights.

Rape involves rage. The first woman to say, "No!" to a man, was the first woman to feel this rage.[7] He may not have raped that particular woman; but assuredly, in similar situations, women were raped. Now the women felt rage. Dr. Leonard Shlain theorizes that a woman's ability to say, "No!" and mean it "poisoned" the relationship between the sexes. This did not mean that rape was frequent in peacetime. Shlain writes, in Sex, Time and Power, "From an evolutionary point of view, intersex mayhem would be too costly and dangerous to maintain." Humans needed to cooperate to survive (19-25).

Admittedly, men still do rape as a personal act of aggression—a "crime of passion." The aggression, however, has clearly gotten out of hand. More rapes are committed in South Africa than any other country in the world. South Africa is engaged in a war against women and children. Carolyn Dempster, reporting for the BBC News from Johannesburg stated, "It is a fact that a woman born in South Africa has a greater chance of being raped than learning how to read." In 1994—the very year South Africa became a democracy—18,801 cases of rape were reported, and by 2001 that figure had jumped to 24,892. This startling number does not reflect the true picture, because the vast majority of rapes and attempted rapes go unreported, or so Dempster was told by the South African Police Service.

In addition, sexual violence against children has increased four hundred percent (400%) in the past ten years. Sometimes children are even abusing other children. Little babies are not exempt. When 'Baby Tshepang' was raped in the Northern Cape town of Louisvale in October of 2001, she was just nine months old. Baby rape is becoming more common because of the myth that sex with a child or baby will cure AIDS (Dempster). Another mythical excuse for rape is that raping an old woman will bring long life to the rapist! How do men excuse the rape of females between the ages of infancy and old age? Or don't they need an excuse because they simply don't realize how monstrous is their conduct?

Dr. Rachel Jewkes, a senior scientist with the South African Medical Research Council states that the problem stems from the men's attitude toward women. They believe that they are entitled to sex. They don't believe that rape is wrong. Women, in this culture of massive inequalities, don't say "No." Sex is not discussed and sexual violence is tolerated (quoted in Dempster).

Lest we think that only countries in turmoil deny to women and girls their basic human rights, the following incident took place in France:

> The boys [ten teenagers] were patient, standing in line and waiting their turn to rape. Their two victims, girls of 13, were patient, too, never crying out, at least according to neighbors, and enduring the violence and abuse repeatedly over five months. (Sciolino)

The reporter goes on to say that in France gang rape is euphemistically referred to as "tournante," or taking turns. There are no statistics showing the frequency of such rapes, but they occur amongst immigrant housing on the fringe areas of big cities where "teenage boys, many of them loosely organized into gangs, prey on neighborhood girls." Rarely are the perpetrators of such rapes brought to justice.

In the United States, rape is a punishable crime. Jamie Zuieback, spokeswoman for the Rape, Abuse & Incest National Network in Washington, thinks that in some cases rapists should get the death penalty, since the FBI rates the violence of rape second only to murder. Only the state of Louisiana, under a 1995 state law, allows the death penalty for rape of children under the age of twelve. Complicating the issue of child rape is that fact that "93 percent of all juvenile sexual-assault victims knew their attacker" (Axtman). Being responsible for the execution of a relative or family friend may often be just too heavy a burden for a young person to bear. In 1977 the U.S. Supreme Court ruled that the death penalty for the rape of an adult woman was too harsh a punishment. Before that ruling, many states allowed the death penalty in cases of rape.

"Police: Abuse Led to Girl's Suicide" reads the lead story by Newell in the Tucson/Region section of the Arizona Daily Star of May 7, 2004. A sixteen-year-old girl shoots herself with her father's gun, after being sexually abused by him since she was seven or eight years old. Suicide is not an uncommon result of sexual abuse. "A Massachusetts study showed about one-third of high school students who were sexually abused, attempted suicide," reports Bridget Riceci, president and CEO of the Southern Arizona Center Against Sexual Assault (quoted in Newell).

Of course, not all rape victims are girls and women. Appearing in the newspapers with sickening frequency lately, are the stories of child molestation and rape by the Fathers of the Roman Catholic Church. An article by Cooperman and Sun, reporting on the findings of a survey of Catholic dioceses in the United States for the Washington Post, states that "the Roman Catholic Church has removed 218 priests from their positions this year [2002] because of allegations of child sexual abuse, but at least 34 known offenders remain in church jobs." The same survey found that of the 850 U.S. priests accused of sexual abuse of minors since 1960; more than 350 of them had been removed from ministry prior to 2002. Many survey responders, diocesan spokesmen, stated that they didn't know the sex or exact ages of the children being molested. Victims, of whatever sex or age, are left forever scarred by such betrayals of trust.

Another ironic betrayal of trust was recently substantiated in the Democratic Republic (DR) Congo. The peacekeepers were sexually abusing girls as young as thirteen! The Office of Internal Oversight Services, the United Nations (UN) "watchdog," investigated abuse allegations in the Congolese town of Bunia. Of the seventy allegations, seven cases involved UN staff—six of the seven were peacekeepers. The seven cases were "fully substantiated." The investigation found a "pattern of sexual exploitation of women and children," many of whom were under eighteen and as young as thirteen. It is a pattern that is continuing. The victims "were usually given food or small sums of money in return for sex." Children cannot legally consent; it is rape and it is a crime, clearly against UN rules. Mr. Guehenno, the UN's under-secretary-general for peacekeeping believes that the people no longer trust the UN mission (Price, "Group Slams").

Rape in Wartime

Rape by peacekeepers is shocking. Rape during wartime is not. War and rape: these twin evils seem joined at the hip. In recent wars, however, rape has become more frequent, more brutal, and more widespread.

A recent report by the charity, Save the Children, found "more than 120,000 girls and young women have been abducted and pushed into conflict." In addition to serving as soldiers and domestic workers, almost all of them also serve as sex slaves. If by chance some manage to escape and return to their homes, "they are often marginalized and excluded from their communities... viewed as violent, unruly, dirty, or as promiscuous troublemakers." It is even worse if they return pregnant or with children. They must care for their children and protect them with little or no community support ("World Armed Groups").

When we think of war, we think "fighting men," but the women and children fight too. Often they fight against a common enemy alongside the men; always they fight against male brutality and lust.

Lack of army discipline, as was the case in Cambodia, Bangladesh, Cyprus, and Haiti ("Rape of Women"), is to blame for many rapes, but there's more to it than that. Rape has "devolved," into an organized, systematic, tactic of war, terrorizing its victims.

1991-1994: Serbian paramilitary troops used rape systematically as a tactic to encourage Bosnian Muslim women to flee from their land.

1994: In Rwanda, Hutu leaders ordered their troops to rape Tutsi women as an integral part of their genocidal campaign.

1997: Secular women were targeted by Muslim revolutionaries in Algeria and reduced to sex slaves.

1998: Indonesian security forces allegedly raped ethnic Chinese women during a spate of major rioting.

Late 1990's: Serbian military and paramilitary units systematically raped ethnic Albanian Muslim women during the unrest in Kosovo ("Rape of Women").

All rape is a horrible violation of human rights, but rape during the war in Bosnia was particularly offensive and uniquely degrading. Local soldiers and UN troops methodically raped the women, young and old, and girls. The UN troops raped those they pledged to protect! (Gilboa).

"Mass Rape: War on Women," by Dahlia Gilboa, goes on to describe the situation in detail:

> Women and girls were literally the pawns of men in the war in Bosnia; they were the targets not only of reproductive genocide, but also of pedophilia, and reckless sexual perversion. Bosnia became a sexual smorgasbord, where soldiers could satisfy their most vulgar sexual fantasies. They knew that, once the war was over, their actions could be blamed on the widely accepted notion that "soldiers do irrational things in times of war." In addition they could use the cowardly defense of numerous Nazi war criminals: "I was only following orders."

Gilboa tells of "rape camps" designed for the mass rape of women and girls. Hundreds of women, treated worse than animals, with little or no food, were subjected to gang rapes and sodomy. Their tormentors forced many to act in pornographic films.

Though frequently taking the moral high ground, the United States is not without guilt. A research paper submitted by Blackburn and Thomas, states that American troops were told to rape women during the Vietnam War as a way of demoralizing the Vietnamese people.

Stuhldreher, of the Political Science Department, University of Washington, Seattle, corroborates the above assertion by writing, "During the Vietnam war, rape was in fact an all too common occurrence, often described by GI's as SOP—standard operating procedure." Not only is such "procedure" a crime prohibited by the Geneva Convention, it is also punishable by death or imprisonment under Article 120 of the American Uniform Code of Military Justice. Rarely, however, were these rapes reported during the Vietnam War, and those that were, seldom resulted in conviction.

As an additional proof, Kevin Gerard Neill, MPH, writes the following in "Duty, Honor, Rape: Assault Against Women During War":

> The charge that U.S. servicemen committed rape is unquestionable. From the individual rape of barroom girls in Saigon to the mass rape and murder of dozens of civilian women in the village of My Lai, the Criminal Investigative Division of the United States Army is rife with documentation concerning abuses by Americans.

Beyond the brutality of rape, however, was the American military's involvement in the commercial sex business. In order to maintain soldiers' morale in fighting an unpopular war, the Pentagon knowingly allowed the formation of brothels on base camps throughout Vietnam.

American military men also rape their own personnel according to a study done by the Air Force's Pacific command. From the years 2001 to 2003, military authorities received reports of ninety-two cases of rape involving Air Force personnel in the Pacific (Schmitt).

In addition to the findings reported in the above study, "There have been at least 112 reports of sexual misconduct, including rape, in the past eighteen months in the Central Command area of operations, which includes Iraq, Kuwait and Afghanistan. Two-dozen women at Sheppard Air Force Base in Texas have reported to a local rape crisis center that they were assaulted in 2002" (Schmitt).

Women in the military, going through training, are sexually assaulted by their very own instructors! On 21 July 2012, Air Force Staff Sargent Luis Walker, twenty-six years old, was sentenced to twenty years in prison for crimes including rape, adultery, obstruction of justice, and aggravated assault against ten victims. This is nothing new. The Air Force Academy in Colorado nine years ago, dealt with allegations of sexual assault.

Sixteen years ago, twelve Army instructors were accused of abusing recruits at the Aberdeen Proving Ground in Maryland, and twenty-one years ago, we had the infamous "Tailhook Scandal" that took place in a Las Vegas hotel. It involved many Navy and Marine officers alleged to have assaulted at least eighty-three women (David Lerman).

General Mark Welsh, commander of U.S. Air Forces in Europe, sounded a sour note when he said, "We've done a lot of work, and we've made no difference" (Lerman) (According to Defense Department figures, women made up about fourteen percent of the active-duty military force last year.) Obviously, to many men, women in the military are women first, and as such, often targets for sexual assault, and soldiers second.

At a June 29th press conference, Secretary of Defense Leon Panetta stated, "We have no place in the military for sexual assault (Lerman).

Liberia is often wracked by war, and aid workers say that every time war rages in Liberia, women flee through the bush in an attempt to escape rape, but when rebels tried to overthrow warlord President Charles Taylor, they increased the outrage by raping women and girls in their homes. "Wild-eyed men are going door to door, ransacking houses, beating and killing people, and raping any women—or girls—they find." The absence of a court system during this war allows the looters and rapists, who are often "drunk, drugged and disaffected" to avoid any punishment (Zavis).

Rape was the order of the day in the Darfur region of Sudan, reported Nicholas D. Kristof, columnist for the New York Times. Shortly after 4 A.M. on March 12, 2004, over one-thousand Jangaweed, Arab Militia armed and paid by the Sudanese government, stormed into the village of Darfur. Mounted on camels and horses, and supported by government troops in trucks, they aimed to destroy. The object was to make the village uninhabitable. The Jangaweed poisoned wells, blew up dams, and massacred the people. Raping the women was bad enough, but then they further stigmatized them by branding and scarring them ("Atrocities ").

"Arab Militias Raping, Killing Females of All Ages in Sudan," captioned a July 20, 2004 article in the Arizona Daily Star. The opening paragraph is as follows:

> Sudanese Arab militiamen rape women and girls as young as 8 and as old as 80 in the violent campaign intended to hurt, humiliate and drive out black Africans from the troubled region of Darfur ... (A8).

A thirty-seven-year-old victim reports that"… [Jangaweed]…are happy when they rape. They sing when they rape and they tell that we are just slaves and that they can do with us how they wish." Sometimes the women's limbs were broken "to prevent them from escaping rape, abductions, and sexual slavery," reports Amnesty International ("Arab Militias").[8]

About a year later (more than two years after the genocide began in Darfur), Kristof spoke with women refugees in Kalma Camp, a shantytown of one-hundred and ten thousand people. These women risk rape every day as they go to gather firewood. They go, because if the men went, they would be killed; the women are "only raped." Sometimes the women are raped just to humiliate them, but other rapes stem from hatred of their skin color and a desire to "wipe them out" ("In Darfur").

In Darfur, most girls undergo an extreme form of genital mutilation, after which the vagina is stitched shut. The stitching and scar tissue make the act of rape even more violent. Some women are raped with sticks, tearing apart their insides, and one woman was raped with a bayonet. In a four and half month time span, Doctors Without Borders treated almost 500 rapes (Kristof, "In Darfur").

Nobody seems to care, certainly not the government—pregnant rape victims have been imprisoned for adultery. The conflict is over territory and over skin color. The rapes are part of a campaign to drive the people from "Arab Lands." Some women report that their rapists tell them they are raped because they are black and because they "want to finish you people off." Some women are never seen or heard from again (Kristof, "In Darfur").

Conclusion

Rape is not an irrational act; in Bosnia, and often in Darfur, it was a plan for genocide and ethnic cleansing. Always rape is a gross violation of human rights. Gilboa sums it up by writing, "The war on women in Bosnia was truly the rape of humanity."

Whether it is a "battle of the sexes" or a war between tribes or nations, rape is ugly. Rape has been referred to as a "spoil of war"—a reward for "manliness"—paid for by the despoliation of the female body. This aggressive act, this molestation of human rights, is becoming more frequent and more vicious. The blood of its victims may soak the Earth, but it doesn't disappear; the spilled blood cries out for justice.

The THINGS WE DO

Essay 3— The World's Oldest Profession

The need for sex a basic drive;

If not for that, who'd be alive?

Yet satisfaction's hard to find:

When one is cold, the other hot;

When one is there, the other not;

When one is ... only one ...

Barter for sex began the first time a sweaty, victorious, sex-hungry hunter dropped a bloody hunk of red meat at the feet of an iron-starved, nubile female, and she went off with him into the bushes. Whether the sex is legal or illegal, voluntary or forced, as long as there is a demand, there will be a supply. The world's oldest profession deserves to be treated as a legitimate profession and its members accorded all the rights and obligations of other professionals.

Admittedly, many people have trouble thinking clearly about the subject, because of the negative connotations; particularly troublesome is the negative reaction to the words "prostitute" and "prostitution." The mere sight or utterance of these words, and minds seem to just shut down. Therefore, for the sake of this argument, and for the sake of the profession itself, the term "licensed companion," as used by J. D. Robb in the futuristic murder mystery, Naked in Death[9] will denote a service industry worker who trades sex for needed goods, and the profession itself will be referred to as a sexual service industry. These terms will be used in place of the older, more negative, terms whenever possible. With the change in terms, it is hoped that we can now consider the subject with less bias and more logic.

A "licensed" companion implies regulation. Health check-ups would be mandatory, even though some would object on the grounds that it is a violation of their civil rights. The seriousness of sexually transmitted diseases (STDs), especially autoimmune deficiency syndrome (AIDS), gives to health a higher priority than ever. Such check-ups would help curb the spread of sexually transmitted infections, not only between the licensed companion and client, but also between the client and any other intimate contact, such as a spouse.[10] Licensed companions, as workers in the service industry, are not alone in having to follow health and safety regulations. Most service industry businesses are regulated. Restaurant owners and workers have to comply with rules of sanitation, most business have safety regulations, and tobacco shops have to check the ages of their customers, etc.—if you are licensed, expect to be regulated.

Being a "companion" implies friendship and comfort. Many lonely, needy people exist in this world, and many of them are sexually frustrated. Sexual frustration makes for a disharmonious society. This disharmony can take many forms, causing varying degrees of harm to the individual or to society as a whole.

Young, single men, in particular, are frequently sexually frustrated. The three most basic of human needs are water, food, and sex. No one has to tell that to teenaged boys who think about sex almost constantly. "A postpubescent boy's sexual desires nearly drive him mad as his brain soaks in a cranial tub laced with testosterone," writes Dr. Leonard Shlain (139). Fathers of daughters, wouldn't you rather this sex-obsessed boy visit a licensed companion than force himself on your daughter?

Fear of rejection, a very common human fear, or just plain shyness, may keep others from forming a meaningful relationship. With a licensed companion, a person would be more at ease and would feel more in control. The effect could ultimately prove to be therapeutic, allowing the person to gain confidence and go on to form a more fulfilling, stable relationship.

Of course, it is not only single people who suffer sexual frustration. A married person who spouse is very ill, or who may no longer have any interest in sex, may benefit greatly, both mentally and physically, from a licensed companion who can bring relief. Men, in many cases, have a stronger sex drive than women, and they may also want more varied sexual experiences than their mates are willing to give them, causing marital conflict and stress. Then too, it often happens that married couples must be apart for long periods of time. Such couples could take comfort in a licensed companion who would be less of a threat to the marriage than an affair would be.

George Flint, legislative lobbyist for the Nevada Brothel Association, says legalization has an altruistic side. "It's a service to dysfunctional or physically impaired men" (Cruickshank). Our wars have seen to it that we have plenty of them.

There are those who argue that sex is so tied up with emotion, is such a personal thing, that to cold-bloodedly put it on the market—to make it a medium of exchange for life's necessities—would be despicable. People are entitled to food and shelter; they should not have to exchange sex for these basics.

Yet people do exchange very personal things for life's necessities without penalty. People sell their blood, their sperm, and even "room in the womb" for money to buy what they need. People join the army and risk their lives. Though the selling of body parts is illegal, the Internet is used to put out appeals for needed body organs. Does money ever change hands? We really can't be certain. If people can do all these things without it being a crime, why is it wrong for a person to sell sex? Selling sex would be less dangerous to the individual than some of the other things people sell. Restrictions as to age, etc., would need to be put in place much as we now restrict tobacco and alcohol sales.

In addition, if prostitution were legalized, it could be regulated and taxed. In the United States' state of Nevada (United States), where brothels are legal in ten counties, prostitution came close to being taxed in 2001 when the state was facing a budget crunch. Nevada is reconsidering taxing brothels, and brothel owners are for it. They believe "a state tax is a stamp of legitimacy." Assemblywoman Sheila Leslie, though she doesn't believe in legal prostitution, agrees that as a legal business, they should be taxed, and she is willing to tax them (quoted in "Nev. Brothel Owners").

The argument that crime would increase if this "oldest profession" were made legal is baseless. Human nature is such that when there is a demand, people seem not to care overly much where the "supply" is coming from. When drinking alcohol was illegal, not only did crime increase, including abortion and suicide, but we also lost a lot of tax money. The "War on Drugs" goes on and on and on, yet it hasn't seemed to make much of a dent in either the demand or the supply. Those who want it can get it. The National Task Force on Prostitution in the United States, reporting on figures compiled in the 1980s, finds "over one million people … have worked as prostitutes …" And all worked illegally, unless they lived in certain parts of Nevada. Those working illegally are often victims of violence ("Prostitution").

As illegal workers, they were often arrested. Of the arrests made, 70 percent are female, 20 percent male, and 10 percent customers. The Task Force found that "a disproportionate number of prostitutes arrested are women of color; and, although a minority of prostitutes are women of color, a large majority of those sentenced to jail are women of color" (quoted in "Prostitution"). It is the poorest prostitutes who bear the brunt of the punishment, causing a downward spiral that brings ever-greater misery to them and their families. No one seems to care.

The arrests not only hurt those arrested, but they also attack society where it hurts the most: in the wallet. The "average arrest, court and incarceration costs amount to nearly two-thousand dollars ($2,000.00) per arrest; paid for by taxes. Cities spend an average of 7.5 million dollars on prostitution control every year, ranging from a million dollars (Memphis) to twenty-three million dollars (New York)," according to figures compiled in the 1980s ("Prostitution"). If prostitution were a legal business, our overloaded justice system would have more time to handle serious cases, and we'd also gain tax money.

Sexual workers seldom report abuse because their work is an illegal activity. According to one report, clients inflict 60 percent of the abuse against street prostitutes, 20 percent is chalked up to the police, and 20 percent to domestic relationships. A massage parlor owner says over 90 percent of the abuse against some of his workers comes from domestic relationships ("Prostitution"). Violence and the threat of violence is an ever-present problem, as it is for women in general, but decriminalization would, at the very least, give the abused recourse to the law, and turn the police into protectors rather than harassers.

Decriminalization alone will not solve the social and economic problems inherent in this "oldest of professions," but it is a first step, and such a step was approved by the United Nations in a 1949 resolution that favored the decriminalization of prostitution. The resolution was ratified by fifty countries, but not by the United States ("Prostitution"). Yet the trafficking of women and children worldwide, both voluntarily and forced, for sex has steadily grown in volume. A ratified resolution is not worth the paper it is written on if it is not acted upon, nor is decriminalization alone enough.

Article 23 of the "Universal Declaration of Human Rights" has to do with work: "(1) Everyone has the right to work, to free choice of employment, to just and favourable conditions of work and to protection against unemployment" (BBC World Service). Not only does this article grant an individual the right to work, to choose the kind of work to be done, but it also grants an individual the right to work in favorable conditions. "Favorable conditions" is too abstract for our purposes. To nail these down, we'll look at what "favorable conditions" are in two countries where prostitution is legal, the Netherlands and Germany.

Prostitution in the Netherlands has always been legal, and it is defined as a "legal profession." Since 1996, prostitutes have paid income tax and have been members of the Service Sector Union. They are not registered nor are there mandatory health checks. A prostitute must be at least sixteen, and the age is eighteen if she wants to work in a brothel. Pimping and facilitating is illegal. Cities can regulate prostitution as they see fit, and they often confine it to certain areas (World Sex Guide).

Germany's "favorable conditions" include health insurance availability (since 1997) and free and mandatory health checks (only Bavaria includes HIV testing). Prostitutes have to register, and they do pay income tax, though they are not considered a regular profession. No pimping or advertising is allowed. If they are not paid, they cannot sue; however, if they don't "deliver" after being paid, the client can sue. They do have an organization (HYDRA) providing information on subjects such as AIDS and fighting to get prostitution recognized as a regular profession (World Sex Guide).

In Thailand, prostitution is illegal but rampant. Six hundred and seventy-eight prostitutes agree that decriminalizing and other preventive measures may be possible solutions to the growing problem of prostitution. Their answer to those that think the answer is education, is that "education is not a silver bullet solution"—reducing the supply will not help if demand is not reduced. They say that as long as the double standard exists, prostitution will exist. It is the attitudes of Thai man that are most in need of changing. Thai men consider the visitation of prostitutes a part of the male bonding ritual even after marriage (Jirapinyo).

Dawn Passar, an immigrant from Thailand, representing the Network of Sexwork Projects in Beijing (1995), learned some important things about the needs of sex workers. Her findings are as follows:

1. It is most important that we make sure they have health and legal information.

2. Many people in Beijing spoke about concern about women in prostitution, but their answer was to pass more laws against prostitution.

3. We tried to let people know the more law [sic] against prostitutes and prostitution, the more the authorities will be given the right to abuse them.

4. The words prostitution and trafficking separate women from all women, but actually, we are all together. The words are overused, and the fact that we are all women gets cloudy. The same laws should apply to all of us, women who are immigrants in the garment industry, in restaurant business or who work as dancers in [sic] as prostitutes.

5. What we need is to get rid of some of the laws we have, so that women ... who do the work are legal, and ...able to call the police and file charges against people who abuse them or exploit them.

Rupam Banerjee, in a Reuter's story titled, "South Asia's Prostitutes Gather to Press Rights," reports that over 1,000 prostitutes from India, Nepal, and Bangladesh staged a march to demand protection from what they called "police harassment." The prostitutes gathered to discuss "ways to legalize their business" and ways to prevent AIDS[11] ("Prostitutes' Rights").

Interestingly, the prostitutes' rights group disagrees with the anti-trafficking proponents who want stricter enforcement of current anti-trafficking laws. The prostitutes' rights group believes that this would give "extraordinary" power to police and immigration officials. Instead, prostitutes' rights advocates from many countries proposed alternatives to laws against "immoral traffic." These alternatives include "the enforcement of laws against abuse, kidnapping, etc. [to be] enforced against all those who abuse prostitutes, including traffickers" (quoted in "Prostitutes' Rights").

The sex workers want self-regulation. As a first step, they "called for the establishment of an independent governing board." In Calcutta the prostitutes called for a self-regulatory council that would give them protection, address corruption, and provide legal and health support. This self-regulatory council would replace the police control of prostitutes ("Prostitutes' Rights").

The "Philosophical Overview" produced by a consultative body representing prostitute advocacy groups in South Australia could serve as a guiding document to any group seeking to decriminalize and regulate prostitution. Its values and observations are as follows:

> 1. No person's human or civil rights should be violated on the basis of their trade, occupation, work, calling or profession.

2. No law has ever succeeded in stopping prostitution.

3. Prostitution is the provision of sexual services for negotiated payment between consenting adults. So defined, prostitution is a service industry like any other in which people exchange skills for money or other reward. People who choose to engage in prostitution have the right to do so under the full protection of the law.

4. Non-consenting adults and all children forced into sexual activity (commercial or otherwise) deserve the full protection of the law and perpetrators deserve full punishment by the law.

5. Workers in the sex industry deserve the same rights as workers in any other trade, including the right to legal protection from crimes such as sexual harassment, sexual abuse and rape.

6. Workers in the sex industry have the right to declare sex work as a legitimate vocation and source of income to financial institutions including lending organizations, credit facilities and the Australian Taxation Office.

7. Individuals and groups who believe prostitution is "wrong" have the right not to engage in prostitution, as workers or as clients.

8. There are some unscrupulous people in all walks of life-government, law, journalism, banking, law enforcement, the stock exchange, medicine, the clergy, prostitution, etc. If every profession were criminalised when some of its members broke the law, there would be few legally sanctioned professions. Unscrupulous people should be summarily dealt with by the law, regardless of

which profession they corrupt. ("Committee to Decriminalise")

The above "Philosophical Overview," if kept firmly in mind as regulations are formulated, could not help but produce "favorable conditions" in the sex worker industry.

Conditions were far from favorable In the Sunset District of San Francisco, on 14 January 2004, as federal agents "busted a sophisticated international prostitution ring in which Asian women were allegedly smuggled into the United States and forced to pay off a forty-thousand dollar ($40,000) debt to their traffickers by selling their bodies." At about the same time the Sex Workers Outreach Project (SWOP) had been lobbying to repeal Bay Area laws that criminalize sex work. If the industry were decriminalized, "Sex workers can report abuse without fear of arrest and customers won't support criminal syndicates." SWOP likes the Australian plan for decriminalization because this would allow sex workers to go into business for themselves (Harrison).

Conclusion

Though the minds of some recoil from the very thought of decriminalizing "the world's oldest profession," prohibiting it has not worked; it has only brought pain and misery, usually to the poorest people. Several benefits would result if it were decriminalized and considered a small business.

First, and most importantly, it could be regulated. Health checks could be mandated, age restrictions imposed, and zoning laws applied.

Second, our over-burdened law enforcement agencies would be freed up to deal with important crimes.

Third, women who were forced into prostitution or who were abused could ask for help and protection without fear of abuse from law enforcement agencies.

Fourth, as a small business, such sex workers would pay taxes; they would also be able to buy insurance, take out loans, and better control their lives.

When there is demand, someone will supply. It's a fact of life. We need to decriminalize it, regulate it, and protect the rights of those who exercise their right to choose this way of making a living. It is as the prostitute, Aldonza, sings on stage in Man of LaMancha:

> I do not like you or your brother.
> I do not like the life I live.
> But I am me, I am Aldonza,
> And what I give, I choose to give.

Essay 4— SUFFER! Little Children

> Hush-a-bye, baby
>
> In the tree top.
>
> When the wind blows,
>
> The cradle will rock.
>
> When the bough breaks,
>
> The cradle will fall,
>
> And down will come baby,
>
> Cradle and all.
>
> (Nursery rhyme, author unknown)

In the past, family trees were broader and leafier, with deep roots, able to withstand whatever fate blew in. Babies were then born at home, in the bosom of the family, and put to the breast shortly thereafter. Mother and baby bonded, and thus the trauma of birth was eased for both of them. Babies also had more people to love and care for them. Unfortunately, few extended families exist nowadays; people move from one place to another like dandelion seeds blown on the wind. Babies, once lovingly birthed at home, now are usually birthed under the glaring lights of a hospital delivery room

The past is gone forever, and in some ways it's a good thing. For example, we've learned the value of sanitation, of vaccination, and of inoculation. Today more people in the world are educated. Electricity makes many lives easier, and modern agricultural methods have increased the world's food supplies. Yes, the modern age has many things going for it, but it has one huge, vitally important drawback: our children are suffering.

In our desire to be "up-to-date," we have, as the saying goes, "thrown out the baby with the bath water." We must rescue our babies. To do this, it is necessary to change the way we birth our children.

Birthing: Past and Present

For tens of thousands of years, mothers bore their children with the help of other women, often called midwives. Birth was a natural process, not an illness needing hospitalization. Things began go awry with the invention of forceps in early-seventeenth century France. Forceps, being a "machine," needed a man to operate it, right? The "operator" more conveniently used the "machine" with the woman lying down on a bed that was really a modified surgical table. Her legs were often secured in surgical stirrups.

"For twenty-five years," says Marsden Wagner, M.D., "we have known scientifically that this is the worst of all possible positions." In this position, the baby gets less blood and oxygen because its head is compressing the main blood vessel that supplies the womb. A vertical position gives more blood and oxygen to the baby, opens up the mother's bony pelvis more effectively, and gravity works with her instead of against her ("Technology"). All good reasons for a vertical birth, but not good enough for the attending physician; a horizontal position on a high table was more convenient. In time, the position became fashionable, forceps gained in popularity, and, as they say, "The rest is history." The obstetrical profession controlled this most important of dramas and the mother became only a bit player, and a passive one at that.

Drugs can be used to "pacify" an anxious mother, but as they enter her bloodstream, they may also affect the baby. It was hoped that epidural anesthesia would be the perfect answer, allowing the woman to be awake but to experience little pain. It was not to be: the baby absorbed the anesthetic from the mother's bloodstream, and often ran a mild fever, requiring separation from the mother for several days (Callander).

Between 50 and 80 percent of hospital births involve surgical procedures: drugs used to start or speed up labor; episiotomies to widen the vaginal opening by cutting the genitals; metal forceps or vacuum extraction on the baby's head to pull the baby out; or a

Caesarean section to cut the baby out. None of these procedures is necessary in at least 80 percent of births. Surgical procedures are always risky. In fact, "the high frequency of their unnecessary use in physician-attended births leads to more dead and damaged babies than would ever occur in midwife-attended births. An example of a frequently used and unnecessary surgical procedure is the episiotomy. According to Wagner, it is used in one-half to three-fourths of first-time births in the hospital, but is actually needed by less than 20 percent of women—the best rate being five percent (Wagner, "Technology").

An episiotomy is not as benign as doctors would like us to believe. It means, "more bleeding, more pain, more permanent deformity of the vagina, and more painful sexual intercourse for months, or even years." When used unnecessarily, it is a form of sexual abuse (Wagner, "Technology"). Birth is a natural process, seldom needing surgical procedures.

Midwives understand that giving birth is a natural process, while doctors are usually looking for the unnatural, the abnormal. Wagner suggests "having a highly trained surgeon obstetrician assist at your birth is about as sensible as having a pediatric surgeon as a baby sitter for your healthy two–year-old when you go out in the evening." Like the obstetrician who speeds up a normal birth with a shot, the pediatrician gives the rambunctious child a shot to hurry sleep. In the first case we have a medicalized "normal" birth: and in the second, we've medicalized normal two-year-old behavior (Wagner, "Technology").

The artificiality of "modern" birthing methods is injurious to both mother and baby. It's time for mothers to regain control. Regaining control means the mother has control over where she has her baby, and sometimes she may decide in favor of a hospital birth with good reason. It is true that some births—about five percent—are high-risk and a hospital with an attending obstetrician is best. A high-risk birth may also require a Caesarean section. The Caesarean section birth rate should naturally be set at just under that of the high-risk rate (around five percent, according to Wagner); but an article in the Arizona Daily Star reports that "more than a quarter of the babies delivered in the United States last year, were delivered by Caesarean section" (quoted in "Caesarean Delivery"). Many of these were not an emergency; they were "elected." The United States is a nation that likes convenience and control. A Caesarean section fulfills the convenience and control criteria for the mother and the doctor, but what about the baby?

A baby delivered by Caesarean section, a major surgical procedure, is disadvantaged from the start. First, the mortality rate is two or three times greater than that of the vaginally delivered baby; if the Caesarean was elected, the rate of mortality is two percent higher. An emergency Caesarean carries with it a mortality rate nineteen percent higher than in a vaginal delivery. Second, hyaline membrane disease is ten times more frequent in Caesarean-delivered babies. Third, pediatricians expect a greater lethargy, diminished reactive response, and less crying in the Caesarean-delivered babies (Montagu, 52, 3). Some Caesarean births cannot be avoided, but if a Caesarean is elected simply because of convenience and control factors, ignoring the disadvantages to the baby, it says a lot about the culture's, and the mother's, priorities.

Montagu, in his book, *Touching*, speculates "had the cesarean-delivered babies been given an adequate amount of caressing for some days after they were born, a significant change might have been observed in their behavioral and physical development" (53). By that he means they would exhibit less lethargy, improved reactive response, and be more contented babies if touched more.[12]

Breastfeeding
Admittedly, there is a place, though small, for hospital births. The five percent of births that are high-risk should take place in a

hospital. This means, however, that 95 percent are NON high-risk births, and are, indeed, natural occurrences and do not need to occur in a hospital—a place for the sick. Birth is the woman's arena. It is her body; she deserves to be in control. She needs the encouragement and kindness of her sisters, and especially of an experienced midwife[13] who puts the child on the mother's stomach —a skin-to-skin introduction of one to the other—right after birth, and as soon as possible thereafter the baby is put to the breast to bond with the mother. [Perhaps the American male's inordinate fascination with the female breast is actually a longing for something he did not get as an infant. Being it's too late for the intended use, he makes playthings of them.]

According to Alice Miller, "It is in those first few minutes and hours after birth that the presence of the infant arouses and encourages the mother's caring capacity, so essential for her bonding with the child (Banished, 85). Furthermore, if the mother is to breastfeed, this is also the time to put the baby to her breast.

We are aware that not all babies can be breastfed. A mother, for various reasons, may need to bottle-feed her baby. So before we sing the very real advantages of breastfeeding, those mothers who can't need not despair. Bottle feeding, if done with extra handling and eye contact, can overcome the developmental setbacks. And, according to Joseph Chilton Pearce in his book,

Evolution's End, separating mother and infant after birth is far more damaging than not breastfeeding:

> It takes an average of 45 minutes for the shock of separation [from the mother following birth in a hospital] to bring on conscious withdrawal in the newborn. It takes an average of ten weeks before the minimal handling, casual physical stimulus, and occasional eye contact many bottle-fed infants receive can begin to compensate for the loss and for a tentative consciousness to reappear. It takes almost three months before the visual system gets enough stimuli to begin functioning again and before the infant smiles. (123, 4)

Babies have been breastfed for more than five million years. It has stood the test of time; it is the best. It provides "immunological, neural, psychological, and organic benefits" (Montagu, 68). Since World War II, however, "97 percent" of infants in the United States have been bottle-fed (Pearce, Evolution's End, 124). Adds UNICEF (United Nations Children's Fund):

> It has been estimated that improved breastfeeding practices could save some 1.5 million children a year. Yet few of the 129 million babies born each year receive optimal breastfeeding and some are not breastfed at all … Professional and commercial influences combine to discourage breastfeeding, as do continued gaps in maternity legislation ("Breastfeeding").

Montagu has this to say about the importance of breastfeeding and of touch, which he deems more of a basic need than sex (192):

> At birth each clearly requires the reassurance of the other's presence. The reassurance for the mother lies in the sight of her baby, its first cry, and in its closeness to her body. For the baby it consists in the contact with and warmth of the mother's body. The support in her cradled arms, the caressing, the cutaneous [skin] stimulation it receives, and the sucking at her breast, the welcome into "the bosom of the family." (63)

Pearce also believes in the necessity for close contact between mother and baby as soon as possible: "Home base at left breast takes care of everything … Proximity with the mother's heartbeat is the number one priority in bonding and the major signal shutting off the stress hormones" (Evolution's, 112).

A recent discovery, reports Shlain, indicates that as soon as the newborn begins nursing, it activates a reflex that causes the mother to "fall in love with her baby":

> Breast-feeding causes nerve impulses to leap away from her nipple and travel to her brain's limbic system. This stimulus causes the amygdala, a major component of the emotional brain, to release a flood of the hormone, oxytocin, which then inundates all the synapses of her nervous system. Oxytocin is the "love hormone," and high levels are associated with the bliss of profound attachment. (82)

The skin-on-skin touching that accompanies nursing has the added benefit of stimulating the infant's five senses.[14] The newborn is genetically encoded to respond to a face, and at left breast, "home base," it is at just the right distance to do so. Recognition of the mother's face sets in motion "the entire visual process." Nursing also immediately awakens the sense of taste. The nerve endings of touch are partially awakened by the touch of the breast, but more is needed. Mammals lick their newborns vigorously for the first twenty-four to forty-eight hours after birth. They do this to insure that all nerve endings are activated. Failure to do so leads to "impaired muscular movements, curtailed sensory intake, and a variety of emotional disturbances and learning deficits." Few human mothers would lick their babies, but all babies would benefit from frequent whole body massage. As soon as the amniotic fluid drains from the baby's nasal passages, the infant recognizes the mother's smell. Another sense kicking in, and the mother's speech, heard in the uterus, is now confirmed (Evolution's, 112-15).

Another advantage for breastfeeding is suggested by a recent University of Bristol study. The study found: "Being breastfed as a baby has a beneficial impact on blood pressure." Researchers studied 2,000 children from Denmark and Estonia:

> After taking account of children's differing heights, weights and stages of development, the researchers found babies who had been exclusively breastfed for at least six months had a systolic blood pressure reading on average 1.7mm Hg lower than those who had not. ("Breast Milk")

The longer babies were breastfed, the greater the impact. Research also suggested a reduction in osteoporosis and ovarian cancer in mothers ("Breast Milk"). Isn't it amazing how many wonderful things the seemingly simple act of nursing does?

Bonding Is Crucial

It is unfortunate when a mother can't nurse her baby, but the feeling of abandonment is the true tragedy. The hospital-birthed baby, usually quickly whisked away and put into a nursery just at the time when immediate nursing at the mother's breast is so important, feels abandoned. Not only is the best opportunity for bonding between mother and child lost, but so too is "intelligence, love, care and nurturing." The experience is so devastating, it cripples the child emotionally and psychologically Pearce goes so far as to state that such a premature separation of mother and baby is "a betrayal of the reason for life itself," and is "the really major disaster of history." (Pearce, Evolution's, 109-24).[15]

Particularly harmful has been the hospital treatment of many black mothers and their babies:

> In 1977 I [Pearce] was sent a thick medical study, begun in New York and then carried throughout the country that showed an underlying hostility by hospital staff toward poor black mothers and babies, who receive far more callous, impersonal, hasty, and minimal care than more affluent white mothers. This uncaring bordered, the report claimed, on sheer brutality, particularly toward the growing ranks of young, black teenage welfare cases. Whatever the psychology, eighty percent of SIDS (silent infant death syndrome) cases occur in the minority poor. (Evolution's, 121, 2)

Horrible as that is, Pearce relates how under the pressure of a timetable, supervisors have told interns to not wait for the afterbirth to normally expel, but to jerk it out of the ghetto mothers, in spite of possible massive hemorrhaging-- another department's concern (Evolution's, 125).

That was more than thirty years ago; let's hope that such immoral, unfair treatment no longer goes on, but even if the treatment of blacks and whites is now equal, it is still a hospital birth, and not as good as a home birth in almost all cases. A 2005 survey of 700 women by The National Childbirth Trust from BBC News, found that a "clinical environment and a lack of space during labor made giving birth more difficult and uncomfortable for many women." Because of the lack of space, a woman could not move freely, leading to a higher rate of emergency Caesarean births. Almost half of those surveyed mentioned their lack of environmental control, including lack of privacy, during labor. An alarming one in twenty-five thought the room in which they gave birth was not clean ("Hospitals Blamed"). That's not all, but it enough to show that hospitals have not been, and are not now, the birthing environment they claim to be.

A baby, born at home and bonded with its mother, has a better chance of survival than the hospital infant. Meryn G. Callander, in 2000, writes: "Statistics show that home births (with prenatal care and a skilled birth attendant) are twice as safe as hospital births, and hold a much better record than hospital births in terms of complications and damage to the baby. Pearce goes even further, stating that a home birthed baby has a "six to one better chance survival" than does the hospital birthed baby, and "so has the mother" (Evolution's, 117).[16]

An ideal birthing outcome is described by French physician Frederick Leboyer: "The newborn child who has come naturally into the world, without destructive intervention, doesn't cry but lies contentedly, even smiling, on the mother's stomach" (quoted in A. Miller, Banished, (84).

A lovely picture but someone is missing, and that is the father. According to Montagu, "there is good evidence that a strong bond of attachment is capable of being formed between father and child within the first few days of its life, and also of being reinforced by his subsequent attention to the infant" (301).

If the baby is born at home, the father should be in the birthing room with the mother. As soon as possible, he, too, should experience skin-to-skin contact with the baby in order to bond during the critical bonding period immediately following birth. Now is also the time to bring in any other members of the family, in order to "lock" all together as they welcome the new baby (Montagu, 111). Such a wonderful experience of family bonding is almost impossible in a hospital birth.

Circumcision

Some consider it an advantage to be in the hospital for the birth of a baby boy. The reason is circumcision; it is a convenience to have it done before the baby leaves the hospital. But why have it done at all? If it is part of the parents' religion, it will be done. But know this: he WILL feel it. Callander, describing hospital birth, says that most males are circumcised a day after birth, and anesthesia is NOT used.

If an EEG (brain-wave recorder) is attached to the infant while the operation is going on, the brain-wave patterns will show "serious disturbance" as he screams. Pearce says that after circumcision, babies do not go to sleep, as parents like to think: they go into shock (Evolution's, 124).

Alice Miller warns against the cruelty of circumcision as it pertains to both girls and boys: Seventy-four million women alive today had their clitorises mutilated when they were girls so that they would never enjoy the sex act. In the case of boys, though the reasons vary from culture to culture, all were circumcised for the best intentions and for the good of the child:

> That this procedure constitutes a cruelty that will later encourage the adult to indulge in similar, also denied, cruelties and will invest his deeds with the legitimacy of a clear conscience is constantly overlooked and ignored, although some scientists have been able to refute all such "reasons" for circumcision ... (Banished, 135).

Desmond Morris tells an interesting account of the original reason for the circumcision of boys:

> The removal of the foreskin ... provided immortality in the shape of life after death. This odd notion was based on the observation that when the snake sheds its skin it emerges with glistening new scales and is "reborn." If the snake can enjoy rebirth by the removal of skin, so too can

the human being. For snake read penis; for snakeskin read foreskin. (quoted in A. Miller, Banished, 136).

If the demands of religion and custom are too strong for the parents of a baby boy to withstand, at least find out if there isn't something that can be done to take away the pain and shock of the circumcision. Circumcision of girls is not to be done, whatever the reason. Alice Miller goes on to say to those adults who torture children:

> He is bound to avenge himself unless his subsequent life allows the old wounds to heal in love, which is seldom the case. As a rule, children who were once injured will later injure their own children, maintaining that their behavior does no harm because their own loving parents did the same. Besides in the case of circumcision it is a religious demand, and to many people it is still unthinkable that religion could demand cruelty. (Banished, 139, 40)

Our Lose-Lose Situation

Concerning the customary hospital birth, the thoughts of Pearce's physician friend from New Zealand, Stephen Taylor, are shockingly on target. He pinpoints the cause and effect of our "lose-lose" situation:

> This is basically a war of man against woman. In the male intellect's long battle with the intelligence of the heart, the real trump card was found in catching the woman when she is most vulnerable and stripping her of

her power. Now, it seems we have her—and are surely had. Beneath it all grows great anger: children angry at their parents; men angry at women because they didn't get what they needed from women at life's most crucial point and still fail to get it; women angry at men for robbing them of their power and, identifying with their oppressors, rejecting motherhood and men in the process. This has caused a rising tide of incompetence and inability to nurture and care for offspring. (Evolution's, 125)

Our children are our future, but what kind of future will angry children create? What kind of future are they creating? Pearce too, has an opinion—a harsh, damning opinion. Though he directs his explanation to the terrible things going on in the black community, much of what he says applies to all communities in which violence, crime, and drug-taking rates have risen alarmingly:

In America, systematic destruction of the bonds between mothers and infants has created a black community at war with itself. Reports of brain damage, estimated as high as 40 percent, from ... [violent] hospital practices have been ignored, and in most cases not even published. The clear and detailed medical studies of autopsies of SIDS victims, 80 percent of whom are black, showing damage due to the violence done to the infant at birth, were ignored.... Black teenagers kill each other with abandon, but there is just as much violence exhibited by black men toward black women, and the anger and fear of women toward their men is all too often taken out on the children.... We blame it all on drugs, of course, or

poverty, neither of which is the case. Our black
communities in the pre-World War II South knew a
poverty far more extreme, harsh, and unrelenting than
today—yet their solidarity and extended family held them
together. The breakdown we witness today is a result of
the violence done both mother and infant at birth—a
psychic shock acted out from that point on. Rather than a
cause, the drug taking we see is in itself but one of the
many fall out effects of this basic genetic damage.
(Evolution's, 127, 8).

Let's hope it is not too late to salvage the future by salvaging

our children. We must start right now to change our birthing

practices. We need to go home. Our hearts know this to be true,

but by now our brains have been so washed by established

medical practices and seemingly painful televised births, that we

are afraid to give birth at home. It demands a lot of courage for

women to go against a society that has, since the beginning of the

1900s, conducted a largely successful campaign to stamp out

midwifery. Growing numbers of women, however, are finding

the courage to "buck" the powerful and hostile medical industry

by choosing to give birth at home.

Re-instating the Midwife

Midwives provide the primary maternity care in

industrialized countries outside North America. In Scandinavia, a

family physician will probably diagnose a pregnancy, but for three-fourths of women so diagnosed, it is the midwife who provides the maternity care. In Sweden, the Caesarean rate is 11 percent; Scandinavian countries have "the lowest maternal and perinatal [the period from three months before birth to one month after] mortality rates in the world" (Wagner, "Midwifery").

Germany has seen a rapid expansion of independent midwifery practice. Home births are becoming far more common, and the numbers of birth centers, staffed by midwives, have increased fivefold (Wagner, "Midwifery").

Wagner goes on to say that in the Netherlands, one-third of births are at home with a midwife, another third of births in the Netherlands, though occurring in a hospital, are midwife-attended. The Caesarean section rate is only nine percent. Unbelievable to North Americans, but true, is that almost every obstetrician in the Netherlands supports this system ("Midwifery").

The National Childbirth Trust (NCT) in England wants more support and information given to pregnant women so they can make informed choices about where to give birth. By not providing this information, Mary Newburn, the NCT's head of policy research, believes the National Health Service (NHS) is being shortsighted, because home births use fewer NHS resources. She would like to see a move toward "more flexible, midwife-led maternity services, based around the needs of women." According to Health Minister Stephen Ladyman, the government is recruiting more midwives, and he adds: "Home birth is a choice that women should have everywhere and we'll move to that position as quickly as practicable" (quoted in "Call for More Help").

Governments have a hard time balancing the budget these days. Savings of eight and one-half billion dollars (8.5B). annually could be realized by the United States by using midwifery for 75 percent of births, says a Johns Hopkins University professor. Eliminating routine EFM (electronic fetal monitoring) would save six hundred and seventy-five million dollars ($675M), and lowering the Caesarean section rate by fifteen percent would be an additional savings of one and one-half billion (1.5B), making a grand total of thirteen to twenty billion dollars (13 to 20B), a year simply by demedicalizing birth! (Cited by Wagner in "Midwifery"). Normal birth, a natural process, does not belong in a hospital, a place where people go when hurt or sick.

For the woman without any serious medical complications during pregnancy, scientific evidence shows that home birth is perfectly safe. Most importantly, the mother will be in control, she'll have the continuous assistance of someone she knows (hospital obstetricians are not always there when they are most needed), and there'll be less unnecessary use of technology. Wagner suggests that to be on the safe side, a mother-to-be should be "within thirty minutes of the nearest hospital," (Wagner,"Technology").

The most important advantage of giving birth at home is that the mother is in control of her own body, but there are other benefits not previously mentioned. Robbie E. Davis-Floyd feels that a home birth often strengthens the family. Wagner, in "Midwifery," points to the overwhelming evidence in the literature, proving the "significantly more satisfying care" midwifery brings to a woman and her family. Wagner, in the same article, suggests that midwives with people skills can successfully "reach the hard to reach, underserved, socially disadvantaged groups."

Helen Fisher, anthropologist, says we may see many more home-births in North America. After being almost wiped out by standardized medicine, along with laws making midwifery illegal in some states, the profession is making a comeback. A growing number of states now permit it, and some hospitals and medical schools train women as professional midwives (First Sex, 136, 7). The Midwifery Education and Accreditation Council (MEAC), founded in 1991, set up ten education programs for direct-entry midwives, and it's also responsible for their evaluation and accreditation (Davis-Floyd).

In most states where direct-entry midwives are "legal, regulated, and licensed, registered, or certified,"[17] and in a handful more where they are either legal or not specifically prohibited, insurance reimbursement from private companies is usually obtainable. Medicaid reimbursement is given in Arkansas, Arizona, Oregon, Florida, Washington, New Mexico, South Carolina, and Vermont (Davis-Floyd).

For those who are still not quite ready to give birth at home, birth centers, where birth is treated as a normal, healthy process, are a compromise solution that is gaining in popularity. If this is your choice, you'll want to find a birth center staffed by midwives, where you can be in control; in other words, one that is not attached to a hospital. Hospitals that have "birth centers," have the hospital and the doctors as supervisors, and doctors rule: not you.

Scientific facts vouch for the safety of freestanding birth centers. Wagner reports on findings from Madera County, California. In the 1960s, midwives were brought in to provide maternity care, where before this care was in the hands of doctors. "A statistically significant drop in the rates of prematurity and neonatal mortality followed." After several years, doctors rebelled, the midwives were fired, and the prematurity and neonatal death rates went back to where they were before the midwives came on the scene ("Midwifery").

A study published in1998, used the whole of the United States to randomly compare midwife and physician attended births. After controlling for social and medical risk factors, researchers concluded:

> The risk of experiencing an infant death was 19 percent lower for certified nurse midwife attended than for physician attended births, the risk of neonatal mortality was 33 percent lower, and the risk of delivering a low birth-weight infant 31 percent lower. (Wagner, "Midwifery").

After considering the above-cited studies and others, Wagner failed to find any evidence that outcomes with midwives were in any way less satisfactory than outcomes with physicians for low-risk women. In fact, "An advantage to midwifery care is that evidence shows primary care by midwives to be as safe or safer than care by physicians" (Wagner, "Midwifery").

Whatever route a mother chooses to go—hospital birth, birthing center, or home birth—it is of vital importance that the newborn immediately has the "loving touch" that will ease the trauma of birth. Alice Miller warns:

> Unless a child receives the warm arms of a person who will console him and tell him with his arms that the shock of birth is over, this child will wait his whole life expecting a repetition of this shock. One of the first lessons is that you are alone, in a dangerous place, and nobody sees your pain. But this situation can easily be changed when we acknowledge the newborn as a feeling and highly sensitive person. Very often the child comes into life after a struggle, and we don't realize that he needs consolation and the arms of a mother. We give him medication, hospitals, and high technology instead. And we think it is good for the child—only because we had the same experience years ago and think it is usual. ("Roots," 20)

So many things that used to be part of a home, have left the home: care of the sick and the old, small industry, animal husbandry, even the growing of food, but the most tragic, is the birthing of babies.

Women have been fooled into thinking that a hospital birth is better than an at-home birth. Usually when a baby is born in a hospital, it is immediately whisked away, when what should happen, and what used to happen when a baby was born at home, was that it was placed on the mother's stomach and as soon as possible thereafter, was put to the mother's breast; those mammary glands are for far more than just looks! An eighty-year-old East African chief recalls his early years and skin contact with his mother, especially with her breast:

> At first she was always there. I can remember the comforting feel of her body as she carried me on her back and the smell of her skin in the hot sun. Everything came from her. When I was hungry or thirsty she would swing me round to where I could reach her full breasts, now when I shut my eyes I feel again with gratitude the sense of well-being that I had when I buried my head in their softness and drank the sweet milk that they gave ... (Montagu, 75)

The effect of this skin-to-skin touching, served to bond mother and baby to the advantage of both. Montagu, in his book, *Touching*, states that skin-to-skin touching is a more basic need than sex. We die if it's lacking. We can survive without sex, so long as some of us are fruitful and multiplying, insuring that we not become extinct.

Conclusion

Birth is natural process. It is not a sickness, needing hospitalization. In addition, mother and baby should bond as soon after the birth as possible. This gives the baby the best chance to be not only physically healthy, but also emotionally and mentally healthy. The easiest and safest place to accomplish this is at home.

It is time for mothers to return home for birthing. As Pearce said, "Home base at left breast [where the baby can hear the mother's beating heart] takes care of everything." It bonds one to the other, and it's best done in the bosom of the family.

> So long as little children are allowed to suffer,
> There is no true love in this world.
> --Isadora Duncan

Essay 5—Our Violent Spawn

> Speak roughly to your little boy,
> And beat him when he sneezes,
> He only does it to annoy,
> Because he knows it teases
> --*Alice in Wonderland* by Lewis Carroll

"[Our] attitude toward infants will either make them good, loving, and trusting or hating and destructive" (Alice Miller, "Roots"). It seems that many have opted for to produce the latter. Too many of our children are violent, depressed, drug-dependent, and suicidal. Our young have run amok. They don't come into the world with these self-destructive tendencies. "So-called difficult, 'insufferable' children have been turned into such by adults. Not always by their own parents. Obstetrical and postpartum practices in many hospitals are often the first to contribute in large measure to this process" (Miller, Banished, 191).

How we treat infants from the moment of birth is vitally important. The essay, "Suffer! Little Children," stressed the value of home births. When a baby is born at home, the baby and mother can easily bond; this is difficult in a hospital birth, where they usually whisk away the newborn. Bonding eases the trauma of birth for both mother and baby—the baby does not feel abandoned, and the mother begins to "fall in love" with her baby, especially if it almost immediately begins to nurse.

When home births become the common choice, we will be on our way to slowing down our presently escalating and disastrous storm of violence. More, however, is needed: the violence must not only slow down, but stop. Only by radically changing our child rearing methods can we hope to accomplish this.

What about Instinct?

Many think that rearing children is instinctual. We are born knowing how to care for our children; after all, parents have been doing it for eons. We give ourselves too much credit. Actually, humans have very little if any "instinctual" knowledge left. Joseph Chilton Pearce declares: "Mothers have lost the knowledge of how to mother due to the arrogance of the male intellect in undermining Mother Nature (*Evolution's End*, 129), and though Leonard Shlain in *Sex, Time and Power*, says nursing releases the "love hormone," oxytocin, causing a mother to "fall in love" with her baby (82), love alone does not insure successful child rearing, it must be coupled with knowledge.

For those who still believe in instinctual knowledge, perhaps this true account of "love" between two zoo gorillas may change their minds. Dawn Prince-Hughes, in her book *Gorillas Among Us*, tells the story of Binami, a female gorilla captured as an infant and zoo-raised, having as playmates chimpanzees and an orangutan. When Binami was eight years old, she was sent to another zoo to become part of a captive gorilla-breeding project. It was hoped that she'd mate with Adhama, a ten-year-old male. But, though both were ready, they could not complete the complex rituals that lead to successful gorilla mating—they didn't know how; they had no older troop members to observe going through the behavior. Someone got the bright idea of showing Binami and Adhama videos of gorilla courtship and mating when Binami next went into estrus. It worked, and in due time, Binami gave birth to little Taufiki (13-14).

That's not all. Gorillas also learn much about mothering through observation. But here again, there were no role models. This time, Karin, a zoo employee, worked with Binami, using a toy, stuffed gorilla to show her how to hold and infant and bring it to her chest. Again, Binami was a successful learner (Prince-Hughes, 15).

A final argument against the existence of a human child rearing instinct, is the fact that humans can produce widely different cultures, depending on how the children are reared. Ashley Montagu writes about two studies done by Margaret Mead in the 1930s:

> The Arapesh children are always being held by someone. The infant is carried by the mother in a small net bag suspended from her forehead. A child's crying is a thing to be avoided, the breast being immediately given to comfort it. Breastfeeding is continued for three or four years...

> Half an hour's cuddling, and the child will follow anyone anywhere. The response to demonstrative affection is immediate ...the Arapesh child grows up with a complete sense of emotional security in the care of others. The result is an easy, gentle, receptive, unaggressive adult personality, and a society in which competitive or aggressive games are unknown and in which warfare, in the sense of organized expeditions to plunder, conquer, kill, or attain glory, is absent. (256-7)

Keep the Arapesh people in mind and contrast their child rearing practices with those of the Mundugumor, living to the south of the Arapesh:

> Even before [the Mundugumor] child is born there is much discussion as to whether it shall be saved or not ... in Mundugumor society the child lives an unloved life ... There is no playful fondling between mother and child. The moment suckling stops, the child is returned to his prison. ["Prison" is a harsh, stiff basket suspended from the mother's forehead.] Children therefore develop a strong fighting attitude, holding on to the nipple as firmly as possible, frequently choking from swallowing too

rapidly. The choking angers the mother and infuriates the child, thus further turning the suckling experience into one of anger and frustration, struggle and hostility ... (Montagu, 257-8).

As a result of such child rearing, the Mundugumor "are an aggressive, hostile people who live among themselves in a state of mutual distrust and uncomfortableness" (Montagu, 257).

If instinct directed child rearing, two such different cultures would be impossible. Instinct is extinct, if we ever had it in the first place. Humans are like the gorillas, Binami and Adhama; we learn by observation, and it stands to reason that we will observe the people closest to us. Thus, we learn to parent from our parents.

Have our forefathers and foremothers created a society that is most like the Arapesh or most like the Mundugumor? Think about it.

A World of Violence

Violence is a constant fact in the lives of too many adults and children—murders, rapes, suicides, abuse, and armed conflicts—and it is increasing. Many would agree that violence is evil, and according to Miller, it is an acquired evil, and is not the reverse of good, but the destroyer of good: "The so-called bad child becomes a bad adult and eventually creates a bad world. The loved child will create a different world … we are daily producing more evil and, with it, an ocean of suffering for millions that is absolutely avoidable" (*Banished*, 142-3).

A Sudanese proverb goes like this: "The world we live in is the world we created." Parents desperately need knowledge about how to love and rear a child so that their children will not repeat generations of past mistakes. It is in this way we really can create a better world.

Children blindly accept their parents' faults without complaint, repressing knowledge of them, because they need their parents' love in order to survive. In fact they often falsely believe that the fault lies in them! In the TV series Lost, Sawyer says to Jack, whose father had emotionally abused him: "Kids are like dogs; the more you kick them around the more they think they've done something wrong."

Parents will often do cruel things to their children under the guise of love—"It's for your own good" (that I hurt you), but such cruelty is actually the opposite of love. Presenting cruel acts as acts of love serve to reinforce the traumatic effect, and further injure the child (Miller, *Banished*, 33). Enough physical or psychical abuse, and the self-fulfilling prophecy comes into play;

the "bad" child grows up to do bad things—what else could be expected? Not only are others disrespected, but so is the self: "The way we are treated as small children is the way we treat ourselves the rest of our lives: with cruelty or with tenderness and protection. We often impose our most agonizing suffering upon ourselves, and then turn around and impose it on our children" (Miller, Roots).

We must admit that our parents made mistakes, painful as that may be, but take comfort in the fact that they are not wholly to blame. Abusive child rearing practices go back through generations. The abuse may be physical, causing injury by cruel treatment or it may be psychical, speaking harshly or using words of contempt to insult or revile the child. Pearce believes that abuse can start at the moment of birth, if the birth took place in a "modern" hospital. In such a hospital, the baby is separated from the mother, rather than being allowed to bond with her, and this, asserts Pearce, makes of our children, "damaged goods" (*Evolution's End*, 170-1).

It's ironic how much attention we pay to our Intelligence Quotient (IQ) in contrast to our emotional intelligence. We can blow the world to smithereens with the touch of a button, but when it comes to controlling our emotions in a responsible way, most of us are clueless. What dangerous toys we "grown up" children have! It's as if our emotions hopped on a runaway train—destination disaster—and there seems to be no way to stop, because we learn behavior by observation, and that's the behavior we've seen, and the behavior our children now see. It is a vicious cycle that has caused untold heartache and devastation through the ages.

According to Pearce, "Close to a million children a year receive medical attention ... from beatings and maltreatment, and some five thousand or so a year die. The average age of the victims is between two weeks and two years. Sexual abuse of children has likewise proliferated[18]..." (*Evolution's End*, 199).

Henry Kempe, of the University of Colorado Medical School, says the attitude of the mother at the time of the baby's birth is the most important indicator as to whether or not a child will be abused. If she doesn't smile, shows no interest in seeing and holding the baby, and if the father's attitude mirrors hers, it is imperative that they have help in raising the child (quoted in Montagu).

Miller, in *Banished Knowledge*, quotes the beliefs, based on the most recent studies of Elizabeth Trube-Becker, a specialist in forensic medicine:

For every reported case of sexual abuse of children there are fifty unreported cases to be assumed. If we add the physical and psychic abuses not primarily sexual, we arrive at the unavoidable conclusion that crimes against children represent the most frequent of all types of crime. (65)

Trube-Becker's conclusion about the extent of sexual abuse shows us to be a nation of bullies beating up on our children— SHAME! Parents often use punishment to "teach a child a lesson," but they are misguided. Miller declares "No one learns anything by punishment. What you learn is how to avoid punishment by lies and how to punish a child twenty to thirty years later" (Miller, *Roots*). Punishment only serves to perpetuate the "same old, same old."

Ron Rolheiser, OMI, writes:

We can never overstate the utter devastation of soul that is caused in a victim of sexual abuse. Nothing so scars, violates and unravels

The soul—literally pulls it apart—as does sexual abuse. I've heard two highly respected psychiatrists say that their hunch is that teenage suicide, so rampant in our culture, is 80 percent of the time a result of sexual abuse … Sexual abuse scars deeply and permanently.

Rolheiser estimates the number of abused girls and boys in the Western world to be one out of every four or five. That means one out of every four or five persons grows up to be a scarred adult. Statistically, "Some form of sexual abuse is happening in every fourth or fifth house in the Western world." He is not excusing guilty priests, who have so often made the headlines, but he says they are "less than .01 percent of this massive problem." While some dispute the axiom, "Every abuser was first abused," all agree that every abuser suffered childhood trauma.

Childhood trauma and lack of the right kind of emotional support seem to be fueling a rising rate of self-harm among young people. A United Kingdom (UK) study, sampling the communities of Hawton, Rodham, Evans, and Weatherall in 2002, found that "6.9 percent of a school population of fifteen and sixteen year-olds had engaged in an act of deliberate self-harm in the previous year"—12.6 percent needed hospitalization. A United States1990 sample, from Centers for Disease Control, showed similar figures for self-harm among high school students (Swales). Though self-harming is relatively common, it is not really understood. The UK is at present in the middle of a two-year national inquiry about self-harm, seeking to understand this kind of self-abuse ("Inquiry").

It is not only young people that self-harm. Olympic double gold medalist, Katie Holmes, revealed that for two months prior to her win in Athens, she had self-harmed by cutting herself with scissors. Leg injuries made her training sessions constant agony.

She said she "felt cursed," and that it was "the lowest I've ever, ever been." Further, "I made a cut for every day I'd been injured. With each one I felt I was punishing myself but at the same time I felt a sense of release that drove me to do it again and again." She saw a doctor for her problem, but with her Olympic success, she says she doubts she'll ever succumb to self-harm again.

The one thing people who self-harm have in common is the experience of childhood trauma. It may have been "physical abuse, sexual abuse, severe emotional abuse, repeated surgery and/or invasive medical treatment, and other forms of trauma such as witnessing violence." Whatever kind of abuse, it was traumatic enough for the victims to hurt themselves ("Trauma").

Child abuse has been a secret part of almost all societies for a long time. Today we are finally admitting its existence and beginning to acknowledge the harm it does. In order to actually survive, the child reacts to the trauma of abuse by repressing the memory and denying the pain of the abuse, which in turn results in neurosis and psychosis. "The child's anger and all the other feelings we don't like are reactions to child abuse" (Miller, *Roots*). Miller warns us: "Many people still have no idea that they are placing dynamite in our world when they abuse their children physically or even 'only' psychically" (*Banished*, 4).

Alleged child-on-child sexual offences at La Frontera, Inc., a daycare facility and school, has resulted in a change of policy; no longer will all the emotionally troubled children be grouped together in the same classroom, as has been the practice. Since 1997, police have been called investigate seven incidents, one assault involved a child of two. A lawsuit is filed against the school and another is pending (Chesnick).

Marianne Martinez, KOLD News Reporter (Tucson, AZ), tells of the babies and toddlers residing at Casa De Los Niños. Angry and aggressive, they are victims of abuse and neglect, according to Susie Huhn, the Casa's executive director. She adds that many will continue the cycle of abuse, ending up as criminals. Martinez ends her report by quoting Huhn: "We know that we can spend $3,000 and do home visitation to a new mom and get her on the right track or we can spend $30,000 and pay for annual incarceration rates for adults."

All children, especially if they tend to be loners, can easily become abused by bullies, themselves victims of abuse. According to statistics:

> 1. One out of four kids is bullied.
> 2. One out of five kids admits to being a bully or doing some "bullying."

3. Eight percent of students miss one day of class per month for fear of bullies.

4. Forty-three percent fear harassment in the bathroom at school.

5. One hundred thousand (100,000) students carry a gun to school

6. Twenty-eight percent of youths who carry weapons have witnessed violence at home.

7. Two hundred and eight-two thousand (282,000) students are physically attacked in secondary schools each month.

8. More youth violence occurs on school grounds as opposed to on the way to school.

9. Eighty percent of the time, an argument with a bully will end up in a physical fight. ("Taking the Bully")

Simone Stall, twelve years old, wasn't arguing with a bully while riding the bus to school in February of 2004. He was sitting in his seat, minding his own business, when some students started beating him. A surveillance camera on the bus caught the action of those doing the beating and of those just standing around, watching ("Camera Captures").

Miller believes that by repressing suffering we become unable to empathize, to feel the suffering and pain of others (*Banished*, 13). The bullies and the watchers on the bus seemed not to care one iota about what Simone was feeling. Unable to empathize, to feel the pain of others, they were entirely capable of cruelty.

A baby must feel protected and wanted, be responded to in a loving way, and of course have the basic needs of hunger and thirst satisfied. When a baby's cries and screams are ignored, believes Miller, distress is repressed, resulting in the diminishment of the ability to ever feel, to be aware, and even to remember the pain (Banished, 13). Children who are not loved, who don't know what love is, can never love others—not even their own children. Statistically, says Miller, a "clear connection [exists] between early neglect and abuse and subsequent adult violence" (*Banished*, 1-3).

Pearce hits us with these disturbing statistics: "Every day 1,512 teenager's drop out of school and 3,288 children run away from home. On any day 1,629 children are in adult jails, while 2,556 children are born out of wedlock (with virtually no support for the mother from any direction" (*Evolution's End*, 196).

Miller goes further "…every murder committed not directly in self-defense but on innocent surrogate objects is the expression of an inner compulsion … to avenge the gross abuse, neglect, and confusion suffered during childhood …" (*Banished*, 26). In a study of about one hundred adolescent males brought into juvenile court, Dr. Hay Helfer found that 85 percent had abusive parents and very negative childhood experiences[19] (cited in Montagu, 306).

A look at crime rates in selected American cities in 2002, show Washington, D.C. experienced 4,854 cases of aggravated assault; Detroit's murder rate was 41.79 murders per 100,000 people (far above the national average of 5.6 for the same year); and Philadelphia, the city of brotherly love, led all other cities in America in its rates for murder, rape, robbery, aggravated assault, larceny/theft, and motor vehicle theft (*Crime*).

Suicide in America is also on the increase. In 2000, 29,350 persons killed themselves. "Suicide deaths outnumber homicide deaths by five to three." Men are more than four times as likely to commit suicide as are women. Among fifteen to twenty-four year-olds, suicide was the third leading cause of death, topped only by unintentional injuries and homicide. Shockingly, among children aged ten to fourteen, suicide was the third leading cause of death ("In Harm's Way").

To help forestall such tragedy, parents can begin laying down the foundation for their baby's self-esteem and security "during pregnancy[20] [emphasis mine] and the first eighteen months after birth when the emotional circuits of the brain are most sensitive to programming," says Olive M. Morton, a psychotherapist of twenty-four years. Her years of working with children convinced her that babies, who do not have their emotional needs met, grow up to be "very angry adolescents and adults." These findings are in accord with those of Pearce, Miller and Montagu. Morton goes on to say, "It is easier to prevent emotional ills in infancy than to pay the extremely high price we are incurring after they become teenagers and adults, by trying to put 'Band-Aids' on this serious problem." If, from the very beginning, the baby's feelings are respected, he or she will grow up to respect the feelings of others.

The Possibility of Change

If we are, as argued, bereft of instinct, and instead learn from observation, we are in big trouble. We are doomed to repeat the child rearing methods taught us by our caregivers and by society. No change is possible.

Not necessarily so. We have made great changes in the past. We started out as hunters and gatherers, became farmers, then later adapted to the Industrial Age, and now we are awash in technology. "All things are possible to him who believes—that is, to him who believes in the possibility" (Pearce, *The Crack in the Cosmic Egg,* 61).

A small group of thoughtful people could change the world. Indeed, it's the only thing that ever has.

--Margaret Mead

Parenting is the most difficult and most important job in the world, and parents can change the world by the way they rear their children.

In the past, parenting was easier. Each home was a "mini" society, but now homes are invaded by outside intruders such as television, telephone/cell phone, and the Internet. Parents need to be strong and put up a united front against unwanted intruders, but it's hard to do in these days of high divorce rates, and even if the parents are married, chances are they both work outside the home. One minute they may be too harsh, and the next too permissive with their children. Parents don't know what to do, and often they are too tired to even think about it. And the stress levels rise for both parents and children.

Some couples would be happier if they decided against parenthood. Men have been the traditional providers, leaving home to go to work; women have been the traditional nurturers, usually staying at home. That's no longer true, more men are becoming nurturers, and many more women are working outside the home, and liking it. Whether or not to have children is the most serious decision of a couple's life. Dr. Heins,[21] author of "Find Out If You Even Like Kids Before Having 'Em," advises those considering parenthood to make an effort to be around children to find out what they are like. Take care of a friend or relative's baby. Volunteer to be a Big Brother or a Big Sister.

Heins' article deals with having "children," plural noun. But it may be best for some to have just one. A University of Pennsylvania study found that people with children are happier than those without. However, "second and third children don't add to the parents' happiness at all" (Krakovsky).

Heins' article includes a checklist that may help a couple decide whether or not they are ready for parenthood. They may find that they have some work to do on themselves first. A partial listing appears below:

1. Do you feel like a grown-up most of the time?

2. Do I know who I am and what I want out of life?

3. Do I feel loved and secure enough so that I am ready to give love to my child?

4. Am I ready for children in terms of my education and career?

5. Can I support and educate a child?

6. Is my relationship ready for a child?

7. Have I resolved, or am I in the process of resolving, any lingering issues with my own parents?

The last two questions require more soul-searching than the others. Having children to "cement" a disintegrating relationship does not work. Childbirth can actually drive a couple further apart. A new baby interferes with a couple's intimacy. Depression can occur in both mother and father, causing them to be unresponsive to their new baby and to each other. John Gottman's studies of newly married couples (some were studied for thirteen years), "show that for 67 percent, childbirth brings conflict, hostility and alienation, that starts many couples down the road to divorce" (quoted in Marano, "Here Comes Trouble").

The question about your relationship with your parents is crucial. Though unacknowledged, the majority of would-be parents today suffered childhood trauma. If they become parents, chances are they will humiliate, scold, and hit their children if that was their childhood experience, and humans learn by observation. There is also an element of "payback" involved: by correcting and disciplining their children as they were so corrected and disciplined, parents discharge their repressed childhood pain. The only way to break the vicious cycle of abuse is for parents, or would-be parents, to recall and feel their childhood pain. By so doing, they rid themselves of the need to inflict pain on their own children, because they will not want their children to suffer as they did (Miller, *Banished*, 29-33).

When a parent abuses a child, physically or verbally, it is confusing. The child thinks: "How can someone that hurts me, love me?" The answer is, they can't. Love flew out the window the moment the parent lost control and caused the child pain. "Love and cruelty are mutually exclusive," and to inflict pain under the guise of love only adds to the trauma. The parent must admit the cruelty, confess that an emotion other than love took over, and apologize. In this way confusion is avoided and the child's self-respect is left intact (Miller, *Banished*, 34-6). It should go without saying that the parent will do everything possible to avoid losing control in the future, such as becoming better informed about the emotional life of a child.

"The child," says Miller, "is not a toy... he is a bundle of needs requiring a great deal of loving care to develop his potential." Perhaps if the parents' bottom line were affected, parenthood would be taken more seriously. Miller puts it this way:

> [Parents] "enter on a commitment to care for the child, to protect him, to satisfy his needs, and not to abuse him. If they fail to fulfill this obligation, they actually

remain in some degree indebted to the child, just as they would remain indebted to a bank after taking up a loan. They remain liable, regardless of whether or not they are aware of the consequences of their actions."

She does not excuse ignorance, for information is available. Once informed, if a couple decides that the responsibility is too great, they must not have children. It sounds harsh, admits Miller, but not if one realizes that an unwanted child is damaged for life (*Banished*, 192-3).

Be careful and choosy about where you get your information. In the past great harm has been done to children because parents believed so-called experts. Consider the banishment of the cradle.

During the 1800's doctors and nurses worried about "overindulging" the child. Lisbeth D. Price, in her textbook on nursing (1892), wrote that the baby "should never be rocked or hushed on the nurse's neck" (quoted in Montagu, 120).

In 1894, Luther Emmett Holt, Sr., Professor of Pediatrics at New York Polyclinic and Columbia University published his booklet, "The Care and Feeding of Children," in 1935. It was in its fifteenth edition. It was a "bough breaker" that brought the baby down, cradle and all." He warned against picking up a crying baby, and advised feeding it by the clock, not on demand.

125

To his credit, he was for breastfeeding, but bottle-feeding was "not discounted." It was a cruel to both mother and baby (Montagu, 78, 120-2).

The misconceptions of the Behaviorists followed Holt's and made things worse. The Behaviorists taught that the only way to study children was through behavior. Their aim was the "encouragement of independence, self-reliance, and the avoidance of any dependence upon the affections of others. One must not spoil children with affection" (quoted in Montagu, 122). What a cold, heartless way to bring up children! Undoubtedly people treated their pets better than their children, and many still do.

Miller believes that Martin Luther's book, *Untertan Kind*, put parents in an "emotional trap." Parents were strongly urged to "chastise and punish their children in God's place; if the parents obey and harshly punish, their children may be damaged; If they disobey, they save their children, while at the same time point an accusing finger at the way their parents treated them! (*Banished*, 198).

Researcher Daniel Goleman explains the three most common "emotionally inept" parenting styles:

1. Ignoring feelings altogether. Such parents treat a child's emotional upset as trivial or a bother, something they should wait to blow over. They fail to use emotional moments as a chance to get closer to the child or to help the child learn lessons in emotional competence.

2. Being too laissez-faire. These parents notice how a child feels, but hold that however a child handles the emotional storm is fine—even, say, hitting. Like those who ignore a child's feelings, these parents rarely step in to try to show their child an alternative emotional response. They try to soothe all upsets, and will, for instance, use bargaining and bribes to get their child to stop being sad or angry.

3. Being contemptuous, showing no respect for how the child feels. Such parents are typically disapproving, harsh in both their criticisms and their punishments. They might, for instance, forbid any display of the child's anger at all, and become punitive at the least sign of irritability. These are the parents who angrily yell at a child who is trying to tell his side of the story, "Don't you talk back to me!" (190-1).

Goleman advises parents to take their children's feelings seriously and try to understand why they are upset. A parent, especially one that is adept at sorting out and understanding his/her own feelings, must help the child find positive ways to deal with upsetting feelings. He suggests such a parent can be an "emotional coach." An effective "coach" will realize extraordinary rewards, according to a University of Washington team study cited by Goleman. Children of "emotionally adept" parents will be:

> 1. More affectionate with their parents and get along better with them; they will also get along better with their peers and be more popular.
>
> 2. Healthier, because understanding their own emotions will decrease aggression and lower stress levels.
>
> 3. More successful in school, because emotionally "savvy" children have increased attention spans; therefore, they become better learners (191-2).

The ideal environment for a child is a home with parents who love each other and demonstrate that love by affectionate touching, and who love their child, and demonstrate that love by affectionate touching. The need for touch, "the satisfying contact or feeling of another's or one's own skin," is universal, and Montagu believes that it is as basic a need as is food and water (77-79, 318).

Infants need to be held and nursed as soon after their birth as possible. The baby carriage should give way to the baby carrier, such as those that may be obtained from La Leche League. An infant needs to be carried on the back of the mother as well as the back of his father. Throughout infancy and childhood, a child needs to receive enough touching, enough loving caresses, for healthy behavioral development to occur. If tender, loving care is not forthcoming, parents may very well be in for some tough times behaviorally in the future (Montagu, 318).

Cultures of the Western world (the United States in particular, says Montagu), need to show more affection—parent for parent and parents for their children. "It is not words, so much as acts, communicating affection and involvement that children, and, indeed, adults, require." These acts of affection become associated not only with the giver's feeling for the recipient, but they also convey a sense of involvement on the part of the giver and give the recipient a feeling of security. Adequate touching, beginning in infancy and carried on through childhood teaches the child how to express affection and how to relate to others. Knowing how to express affection is crucial for successful and satisfying relationships (318-319).

Children reared with love and respect, by parents who love and respect each other; will, in turn, love and respect their parents. (That's what parents want most, isn't it?) This is the ideal family environment—an ideal that is becoming rare. The divorce rate is increasing worldwide. In the United States few marriages last beyond a few years. Indeed, divorce has become almost glamorous—not surprising considering the fact that our role models these days tend to be entertainment figures.

Divorce almost always has a negative effect on children. This is true no matter what their age. "Children of divorce are twice as likely to be abused and to become criminals and teen moms—even if they have stepparents" (quoted in "Americans for Divorce Reform"). The three most common problems are psychological (anxiety, sadness, depression, etc.), poor school grades or grades below ability, and aggression toward parents ("Fatherless Homes").[22] The children from fatherless homes, or homes where the father is the noncustodial parent, are at greater risk for all of the following:

1. Sixty-three percent of youth suicides

2. Seventy-one percent of pregnant teenagers

3. Ninety percent of all homeless and runaway children

4. Seventy percent of juveniles in state-operated institutions

5. Eighty-five percent of all youths setting in prisons

6. Eighty-five percent of all children that exhibit behavioral disorders

7. Eighty percent of rapists motivated with displaced anger

8. Seventy-one percent of all high school dropouts

9. Seventy-five percent of all adolescent patients in chemical abuse centers

("This Is What Happens to Children").

And the beat goes on. We humans learn by observation, remember? Children are watching and learning from their "core protectors": their parents. They develop expectations about how people act and react in relationships. Parents become their "working models of intimacy … a blueprint for adult romantic pairings" (Bower). If children's parents see divorce as the only way to solve marriage problems, it will be what the children will do when they have problems in their marriages. Perhaps squabbling parents could benefit from looking at Goleman's inept parenting styles and see if one corresponds to their partnering style. If one does, they could find themselves an "emotional coach"—they may thereby save not only their marriage, but also the future marriages of their watching children.

What about the many parents who are not married to each other? So many problems exist with just existing for some people today, that marriage gets put on the back burner, if it's considered at all. A Healthy Relationships and Marriage Education course recently begun in Pennsylvania is aimed at unmarried couples with a child under the age of one. Specifically, it promotes marriage as a way out of poverty. Since July 2003, thirty-five couples have taken the twelve-week course; two couples have married and ten have become engaged (Winters). Not only does marriage have economic benefits, it also gives children more security, for "married couples are less apt break up" (quoted in "Trend to").

Fathers have been underutilized and unappreciated. Fathers have a value far beyond that of sperm donor and traditional provider. In the past, fathers were barred from the delivery rooms. In fact, fathers have only a minimum amount of contact with their children in 60 percent of cultures (Lamb).

We all know that some mothers suffer from "baby blues," or postpartum depression following the birth of a baby, but now it's discovered that fathers can also suffer postpartum depression. Bristol and Oxford University doctors found that about ten percent of new fathers suffer from depression, accompanied by "anxiety, mood swings, irritability and feelings of hopelessness" two months after the birth of their first child. Postpartum depression affects the quality of maternal care, so too, does it affect the quality of paternal care. In both cases, children suffer, but a father's postpartum depression affects a baby boy more than a baby girl ("Father's Blues").

Behavioral and emotional problems showing up in the child of a depressed father may become psychiatric disorders in adolescence. Dr. Paul Ramchandani, Oxford psychiatrist, said: "It may be that boys are specifically sensitive to the effects of parenting by fathers, perhaps because of different involvement by fathers with their sons…fathers influence their children's development from very early in life." He added that it was important such feelings in fathers be noted and that fathers be offered the necessary treatment (quoted in "Father's Blues").

American fathers are becoming more involved: "One in four dads takes care of his preschooler during the time the mother is working.[23]

The number of children who are raised by a primary-care father is now more than two million and counting" (Abrams). Even fathers working full-time are more involved with their children than in the past, and a "small but growing number" are cutting back on their work load, or "down-sizing their aspirations" in order to have more time for their children. Most promising of all is "about thirteen percent of U.S. companies with more than one hundred employees offer some paid paternity leave" (Armour).

Paid paternity leave for fathers gives them a change to get to know their baby—to bond. Fathers, as compared to other men, have a high level of the female hormone, estrogen. This change in hormone level occurs during the partner's pregnancy, and most likely, because of it. Nature is preparing both parents for their baby. In fact, the best fathers experience a drop in testosterone after the baby's birth. If the father then regularly interacts with his child, his estrogen level remains high—he is a nurturing, devoted dad (Abrams). While testosterone drives a man to copulate, estrogen helps him nurture the fruitful outcome.

Fathers are more versatile—and valuable—than thought. Unfortunately, fathers sometimes have to be away from their families for extended periods of time—military obligation is a good example. If a father is not present for the birth of his child, or very shortly thereafter, he misses the best bonding time. If his absence is extended, he may have difficulty being a nurturing dad, and should he be absent altogether, his children will surely suffer.

Though true for both sexes, this is especially true in the case of boys. Boys are different from girls. Aside from the obvious anatomical differences, there are innate brain differences, molded by culture after they are born. "You cannot make a girl into a boy or a boy into a girl," says Helen Fisher, quoted in the DVD, "Science of the Sexes." Boys tend to be more active and aggressive than girls. They crave attention and admiration: "Watch me! Look, Dad! See what I can do!" They tend to be less patient and more willing to take risks. They seem to have a hierarchal gene: they want to be "King of the Hill." They also need definite behavior rules and boundaries, which they learn to observe through consequences, not punishment. Above all, they need a caring father who demonstrates self-control and appropriate adult male behavior. Montagu has this to say about behavior toward boys—it's changed, but not enough:

> There has been a great change in the earlier forms of hostile demonstration of "affection" towards boys, but what remains is the expression of anger towards the child in the form of aggressive tactilisms, such as [barbaric] slapping, spanking, or shoving. "Corporal punishment" is still widely practiced throughout the Western world, and the skin not only made a target and a vehicle for the experience of pain, but an organ which is directly associated with anger, punishment, sin, aggression, naughtiness, and evil. (303)

Perhaps we can learn something from Anna Whitehouse's study of elephant behavior. She tells of the orphaned, male elephants that were moved to Pilanesberg National Park, a wild game preserve. After several years of living without normal elephant social structure, and without any adult supervision or discipline, they began killing white rhinos. When a group of adult male elephants were put into the Preserve with them, their violent behavior stopped. Whitehouse concludes, "Adult males are necessary in order to avoid abnormal behavior amongst teenage bulls ..." (50). It's a corollary speaks for itself: sons need good fathers.

Sons may also need less "good-to-them" mothers. In the novel, Morality for Beautiful Girls, one of the main characters, Mma Makutsi, makes this astute observation: "Women, as usual were expected to behave better than men, and inevitably attracted criticism for doing things that men were licensed to do with impunity. It was not fair. It had never been fair ...Men would wiggle out if it somehow, even if you tied them up in a constitution." She wonders why this is so, and comes to the conclusion that it has something to do with the way mothers treat their sons:

> If the mothers allowed the boys to think that they were special—and all mothers did that, as far as Mma Makutsi could make out—then that encouraged boys to... think that women were there to look after them, then they would continue to do this when they grew up—and they did. (Smith, 207)

Mma Makutsi thinks of an example: She saw the mother of an apprentice mechanic come to the garage with a whole watermelon, which she proceeded to cut for him. She then fed him the watermelon as "one would feed a small child." Mma Makutsi did not think the mother should do that; her son should be encouraged to buy his own watermelons and cut them up too. "It was exactly this sort of treatment which made [men] so immature ..." (Smith, 207). A strong, loving MATURE father is the antidote.

A daughter needs a father to be there too. If her father always shows love and respect for her mother—the person with whom she most closely identifies—she will grow up to be a confident women with high self-esteem. This is sorely needed, as a survey of 2,000 girls done for Bliss magazine came to the conclusion that almost all of them "hate their bodies." Many suffered from anorexia or bulimia. Thinness makes a girl not only more popular with boys, but also with girls, thought eighty-eight percent of those surveyed. Psychotherapist Andrea Scherzer, an eating disorder specialist, says: "These girls need to learn to value themselves as individuals first" (quoted in "Teenage Girls"). If a loving father values his daughter from the day she was born and on, she will grow up valuing herself.

A daughter can also learn about relationships from her father and mother. By observing the relationship between her parents, she learns how a man treats a woman. This "first man" in her life will be the standard by which all subsequent men will be judged (Parker).

This "first man" in her life may also delay puberty—a definite plus with the present high rate of teen pregnancy. A study of 173 girls and their families, led by researcher Dr. Bruce Ellis of the university of Canterbury in New Zealand, found that those who have a "close positive family relationship in their first five years—especially with the fathers—enter puberty later in life." Furthermore, these later maturing girls; fathers were their active caregivers and not only had positive relationships with their daughters, but also with the mothers. The father had to be the biological father; the presence of stepfathers or boyfriends of the mother did not have this delay-of-puberty effect (quoted in Parker).

The opposite is true for girls growing up without a father in the home, or in dysfunctional homes with a father. These girls started to menstruate earlier, often becoming sexually active before they were emotionally ready. The reasons for the age differences for the onset of puberty is as yet theory, but whatever the reason, when we consider the prevalence of teen motherhood and of sexually transmitted diseases, anything that delays the onset of puberty is better for everybody (Parker).

Statistics show the number of teen pregnancies in the United States to be the highest by far out of nine "rich" countries, with the United Kingdom coming in second, with LESS THAN HALF the rate per thousand teen as the United States (A Comparison).

The United States has made some improvement. In 2001 the pregnancy rate of "women" under age fourteen was 1.9 per thousand lower than the 1972 rate (5.8 per thousand); also in

2001, the pregnancy rate of women aged fifteen to nineteen was 14.3 per thousand lower than the 1972 rate (39.0 per thousand)—a significant drop among the fifteen to nineteen-year-old age group ("U. S. Teen Pregnancy Statistics"). The rates may have improved some, but not enough by any means.

Julie Atkins, thirty-eight, of Derby, England, would agree that there is lots of room for improvement, especially in her own household. Her three daughters, aged twelve, fourteen, and sixteen, who live with their mother, have all given birth. Mrs. Atkins said they were too young, and that now their lives were ruined. She blamed the schools for "poor quality" sex education ("Sisters Give Birth"). They certainly are too young, but "poor quality" of sex education—if it was poor—is only partly to blame.

Our modern culture provides our young girls with some of the worst possible role models: entertainers flaunting their sexual attitudes, singing suggestive lyrics, hypocritically dressing to look like they're ready to "put out." The American television series, Sex and the City, celebrated the supposed ability of women to take sex as lightly as men. To again quote Fisher (in "Science of the Sexes"), "You cannot make a girl into a boy or a boy into a girl." The sex that gets pregnant, the sex that needs help while pregnant and rearing children, the sex that actually brings forth the future and nourishes it, just cannot take sex as lightly as men. But this is not the message our young people get. In the interests of corporate profits they are encouraged to buy, buy, and buy the tasteless clothes and to always, ALWAYS, be "sexy."

Shortly after the news of the three young sisters all giving birth in Derby, the BBC News came out with this headline: "Parents Must Tackle Teen Births." The British have the highest rate of teenage pregnancies in Western Europe, in spite of government efforts to control it. In the article, the British government admitted that it couldn't do anything more about the problem. Parents had to "put aside any embarrassment" and talk to their children about sex. In fact, though parents should be on the front line for informing children about sex, it is also necessary for teachers, school nurses, and doctors to get involved because of the complexity of the ever-increasing problem[24] ("Parents").

So much stress has been put on freedom and equality in America, but Americans just skim the surface of what "freedom" and "equality" mean, and our consumer culture encourages such shallowness. All girls and women would do well to ponder the words of Syrian writer Ghada Samman: "The liberated woman is not that modern doll who wears make-up and tasteless clothes … The liberated woman is a person who believes that she is as

140

human as a man. The liberated woman does not insist on her freedom so as to abuse it."

Not until women and men are thought of, and treated as, equals by both sexes, will women be able to live their lives according to the wisdom of Samman's words. As long as we live in a patriarchal world, some women, especially the good-looking ones, will not be able to resist the rewards they get by "courting" the favor of those in power.

Women know that men are "beguiled by beauty," and though they may deplore it, women all over the world exploit it (Fisher, First Sex, 233). Men are also more driven by their sex drive. In addition, everyone, male or female, wants attention, especially from those with power and status. Until women have power and status on par with men, why shouldn't they use the avenues to power that they do have? It just makes sense.

Or does it? The saying, "If you've got it, flaunt it," invites a young woman to bare all, or almost all. In so doing it takes away the mystery, and it is the mysterious that is attractive to both men and women. Sex, says Fisher, is a "precious present" that a woman gives to a man (First Sex, 256-283). Giving the same present to many men not only takes away the mystery, it greatly devalues the gift.

A man will usually take what he can get, but if a woman wants a mate, wants a man that will be her true and faithful partner, she had better guard the mystery and not be too generous until she's found a suitable recipient. Now, that is what really makes sense—that the "big picture." But our young girls, in their shortsightedness, are not buying it. Success for the female in America is to be a "successful manipulator of her world" (Montagu, 316), aided and abetted by our consumer culture.

Our media advertising overwhelmingly implies that for a woman, beauty at any price (buy, buy, buy!) is worth it— "Because you're worth it!" Beauty becomes almost everything, eclipsing natural talents and creativity, and beauty is so fleeting!

If a young woman is not beautiful enough to be a manipulator, or doesn't want to play this game, she may just opt out and escape the pain of not belonging by turning to drugs, promiscuity, or self-harm.

If, however, a young woman comes from a loving home where she has been valued and respected for who she is, not how she looks; if she's been encouraged to be all that she can be and not pigeon-holed into any kind of vapid sex role; and if her father has loved and respected her mother, chances are she'll have the confidence and self-esteem to stand against the negative assaults of our skewed society. She can sing along with Avril Lavigne:

" Nobody's Fool"
If you're trying to turn me into someone else,
It's easy to see I'm not down with that.
I'm not nobody's fool.

Strong, loving fathers do much to prevent daughters from being anyone's fool. And strong, loving fathers demonstrate for sons how a real man acts and reacts in the world and in his home. Fathers, you are needed.

Conclusion

Daniel Goleman, author of Emotional Intelligence, predicts a grim future for today's children unless things change. With so much crime and a divorce rate around 50 percent, that he believes will rise even higher, how can our children hope to someday marry and have stable, happy families? (232). Where are their role models? Children learn by observation, and what have they observed?

It's time to change their view. We know, from the widely diverse cultures of the Arapesh and Mundugumor that humans are malleable. We can create a better reality, and we must start by radically changing both our child birthing and our child-rearing methods. Mothers and babies need to bond to ease the trauma of birth. If possible, the father should be present at the birth and also bond with the new baby. Children must no longer suffer abuse, for it only turns them into future abusers: a vicious cycle.

Child abuse is shockingly widespread. When a child's needs are not met, the distress is repressed, and eventually the child will cease to have any feeling-- any empathy or sympathy—for others. Such a child is capable of the most horrendous cruelty. If he has children someday, the abuse will be repeated, for we learn by imitating what we see.

Parents must be helped to recognize what they are really doing and be informed about ways to change. It is essential that they go back and feel the pain of their own abuse in childhood; they will not then want their children to have to experience such pain. They will stop the vicious cycle.

Lastly, we need to find a way to lower our divorce rate, for divorce is not good for children. A loving, secure home, with married parents who know how to meet the needs of a child, is the ideal environment in which to raise a child. Children coming from such homes have the best chance to be physically, mentally, and emotionally healthy. Children coming from such homes can change the world. Raul Seizaz, Brazilian Composer, writes:

"A dream that I dream alone is but only a dream
But a dream that we dream together is reality."

The THINGS WE DO

Essay 6— Educating Reuben and Rachel

Reuben, Reuben, I've been thinking
What a fine world this would be
If the men were all transported
Far beyond the northern sea.

Oh, my goodness, gracious Rachel,
What a strange world this would be
If the men were all transported
Far beyond the northern sea.

Reuben, Reuben, I've been thinking
What a great life girls would lead
If they had no men about them
None to tease them, none to heed.

"Rachel, Rachel, I've been thinking
Life would be so easy then
What a lovely world this would be
If you'd leave it to the men

147

Over 50 years ago, many grade school children in the United States, attending country schools, used to sing the above song. Girls would sing the first verse, the boys the second, keeping to that pattern to the end. Some schools may still sing it, and to girls and boys it is still a tempting proposition, though an impossible one We may not like or understand each other at times, but we need each other. We can't even send each sex back to its respective planet, as per the title of John Gray's book, Men Are from Mars; Women Are from Venus.

Yes, males and females must share planet Earth, but that doesn't mean they have to share a classroom. In fact, both sexes would be better off if they didn't.

Granted, the world is a mix of the sexes, and men and women need to learn how to relate to each other, but in the formative years, especially the years from the onset of puberty, until the brain matures, a process called "myelination,"[25] both sexes have more than enough to do just trying to figure out who they are and how to relate to themselves. Determining the age of brain maturity is a problem. The Supreme Court will not execute people under fifteen for a crime, and plans to consider changing it to eighteen. Reuben Gur, of the University of Pennsylvania said some scientists advise setting the legal age at twenty-two or twenty-three (Bowman).

Complicating this whole process are the innate differences between female and male brains as outlined in the television special, "Science of the Sexes." The two sides of the female brain are better connected than that of the male brain, allowing her to better see the "big picture"; the television special compared her brain to a "floodlight." This better connection also accounts for her greater ability to multi-task.

The male brain, on the other hand, is "more specialized, more compartmentalized," letting him focus more sharply on details; the same television special compared his brain to that of a "spotlight." But this specialization limits his ability to "multi-task"; he does things one at a time. The male is superior at tracking moving objects—the faster, the better, and he is more willing to take risks than is a female. In addition, he has a better sense of space, making him better at navigation.

Through an experiment featuring two toddlers, one boy and one girl, the "Science of the Sexes" television special clearly showed the difference between the sexes when it came to dealing with a physical separation from the mother. In both cases, a barrier separated mother and child. The little boy tried to break down the barrier, while the little girl called for help She used her language skills. The language skills of females are greater than that of males. Males, however, excel at discovering how things work--mechanical skills—but when you get into the finer motor skills, females have the patience and dexterity needed to do better than males.

Females tend to have more empathy, more sympathy and compassion. Where boys want to find out how things work, girls want to find out how people work. The hormone estrogen makes them better at personal relationships

The sexes fight differently. Girls, having better language skills and lacking the muscles of testosterone-fueled boys, fight with words. Boys fight aggressively, pushing and hitting, fueled by testosterone that gives them more energy. Testosterone also feeds their desire for rank and power.

Though males have the testosterone, leading to more muscle mass and strength, especially in the upper bodies, females have greater stamina. Not only do they live longer than males, but they also do better in long-distance contests such as swimming or marathons. They "can pace themselves better." Helen Fisher, anthropologist and expert in gender differences, ended the television special with the admonition that one cannot turn a girl into a boy or a boy into a girl

It's time we took these differences into account in the classroom. It just doesn't make sense to teach girls and boys in

150

the same way or in the same space. We need to stop short-changing our young people. Both males and females would benefit from single-sex education, especially during their formative years, from eleven to about twenty-one, at which time their brains shall have reached maturity.

One major objection to single-sex education is that it doesn't prepare a child for the real world, which is, of course, sexually mixed. On the surface this sounds logical, but we are talking about young people here—young people who are hormones on legs, and who have not developed the strengths and confidence to deal with the "real world." They need time—time that is not spent fending off unwanted advances.

Dowling writes in *The Frailty Myth*, about the 1993 report put out by the American Association of University Women (AAUW), titled "Hostile Hallways." The study reports that 70% of public school girls experience harassment. Whether cornered and molested (25 percent) or victims of unwanted sexual touching (50 percent), it's a devastating experience for the girls. School becomes a place of fear, and many no longer want to go to school (126-133).

Though girls who are taught in a single-sex classroom have just as many heterosexual relationships as girls taught in a coed environment, they have fewer unwanted, teen-age pregnancies. The United States still leads the industrialized world in the number of teen-age pregnancies. Few things have a more detrimental effect on a girl's future plans than an unwanted pregnancy. The girl who attends single-sex classes still deals with boys, but she does it outside of school and with more control, with more independence. She is able to say, "No!" more easily because her social network, her peer pressure group, is most probably separate from her boyfriend's group of friends ("Advantages for Girls"). The control and independence with which she handles her teen-age relationships will be an advantage in her future relationships with men.

The single-sex classroom for boys will also produce men that can more effectively deal with women in the real world. Bruce Cook, Principal of The Southport School on the Gold Coast, Australia, has found that boys in an all-male school have greater confidence when in the presence of girls and "become more sensitive men." Not only that, but they do better academically (West). These qualities will definitely be assets in the real world, not only in dealing with women, but in dealing with people in general. Boys attending single-sex classes come out of them better able to deal with the real world.

Single-sex education, therefore, does prepare our young people for the real world. Yet, in these days of tight educational budgets, some fear that the cost is prohibitive. A real-life success story coming from Thurgood Marshall Elementary School in Seattle, Washington, can speak to that fear. When the principal of this school turned it into a "gender-separate academy," he used no additional funding. His experiment resulted in "students' grades and test scores soaring, disciplinary problems vanishing, and everybody's attitude improving." The press was happy to report these successes, but they often failed to report the careful planning and professional development that paved the way for this success ("Single-Sex Education"). Professional development, an ongoing fact in a teacher's life, just needed a little different focus.

Then there is the biggest objection to single-sex education: segregation means second class. Terry O'Neill, a National Organization for Women vice president is quoted as saying, "We think segregation has historically always resulted in second-class citizens" (Austin). This is a legitimate fear. Think about the treatment of blacks during segregation. Research, however, shows that segregated, or single-sex classrooms, have definite advantages for both sexes.

The National Foundation for Educational Research studied the effect of 2,954 public high schools in England (grades 9-12), a country where there are many single-sex public high schools. The report, released on July 8, 2002, found that both boys and girls did significantly better in single-sex schools than in coed schools. "Girls at all levels of academic ability did better in single-sex schools than in coed schools; whereas for boys, the beneficial effect was significant… at the lower end of the ability scale." In addition, "Girls at single-sex schools were more likely to take non-traditional courses … advanced math and physics" [26](Single-Sex vs. Coed").

A 2001 Australian study, done by The Australian Council for Education Research, compared student performance in single-sex schools with student performance in coed schools. They studied 270,000 students, taking fifty-three academic subjects, over a period of six years. The students in single-sex classrooms "scored on average fifteen to twenty-two percentile ranks higher than did boys and girls in coeducational settings." They also found that boys were happier in the single-sex setting, finding learning more enjoyable and the curriculum more relevant. They were also better behaved. The report concludes: "Evidence suggests that coeducational settings are limited by their capacity to accommodate the large differences in cognitive, social and development growth rates of boys and girls aged between twelve and sixteen" ("Single-Sex vs. Coed").

Marlene Hamilton, studying students in Jamaica, found that "students attending single-sex schools outperformed students in coed school in almost every subject tested." At a time of her study, there were still many single-sex public schools in Jamaica, and so little academic and socioeconomic differences existed between the two types of schools. Hamilton stated, "Girls at single-sex schools attain the highest achievement; boys at single sex schools are next; boys at coed schools are next; and girls at coed schools do worst of all" ("Single-Sex vs. Coed") Single-sex schools clearly win out over coed schools.

If some still fear that single-sex can deteriorate into "second-class," then they should serve on school boards in order to be certain that tests for both sexes are of like difficulty, that there is uniformity of quality in curriculum selection, and above all, that teachers are properly prepared. If this is done, neither sex will get a "second-class" or a "watered-down" education. The proof should be in the SAT scores.

Girls and boys are best taught using different teaching methods. Leonard Sax, founder and executive director of the National Association for Single Sex Public Education (NASSPE), and who is also a family physician with a Ph.D. in psychology, has experienced and researched single-sex education. "The key to a successful single-sex environment," says Sax, "is remembering that there is no difference between what girls and boys do, but there is a difference in how they do it" (Davila). Teachers in single-sex classrooms need to be made aware of the differences in learning styles of girls and boys, so that they can adjust their own teaching styles to best fit the sex they are teaching.

In the not-too distant past, it was assumed that gender differences were largely "culture based." If we only raised children differently, there would not be marked personality differences. Not true, as Dr. Helen Fisher reminds us when she says that one cannot turn a girl into a boy or a boy into a girl. In fact, gender differences exist across all the cultures studied by the National Institutes of Health (NIH): China, sub-Saharan Africa, Malaysia, India, the Philippines, Indonesia, Peru, the United States, and Europe (Croatia, the Netherlands, Belgium, France, Germany, Italy, Norway, Portugal, Spain, Yugoslavia and Western Russia). Surprisingly, it was found that "gender differences were most pronounced in European and American cultures in which traditional sex roles are minimized" ("Learning Style Differences").

Rather than trying to ignore these differences, as coeducation so often does, it is much wiser to use them to each sex's educational advantage, and this is best done in a single-sex classroom. For the girls, this means a place in which they would receive encouragement, for girls tend to very good, sometimes *too* good, at criticizing their own performance. Boys, on the other hand, tend to think they are doing a better job than they really are. They need a "reality check" that will challenge them to do better ("Learning Style Differences").

Another difference is motivation. Girls are more motivated by the idea of pleasing adults than are boys. Boys are motivated by subject matter that interests them. Another important difference, is the way that the sexes react to failure. When girls experience failures, they feel of little worth, because by failing, they have disappointed adults. Boys who experience failures limit their feelings of failure to the subject they've failed. Because they have a "relative lack of concern with pleasing adults," they are more protected from a feeling of self-diminishment (Pomerantz, etal., study quoted in "Learning Style Differences").

Step into a classroom designed for girls, and you'd be entering an orderly, safe, comfortable, and welcoming environment. The noise level would be below that of coed classrooms. (Girls hear two to four times better than boys, especially the softer sounds.) Chairs would be soft Perhaps bean bags would enhance reading areas. If teacher and students were on a "first name basis," it would not cause discipline problems; on the contrary, girls want to think of their teacher as their ally, and this would promote such a feeling. If a new subject were being introduced, it would be preceded by context material— maybe a story or an anecdote. Girls learn better when subjects are introduced by some background information.

Girls also learn well in small-group settings,[27] and role-playing is an extremely effective teaching method for girls. If the subject being taught were literature, it would probably be fiction and be about relationships. Girls like fiction, and like thinking about motivations and behaviors—"how people work." Older girls would enjoy handling questions about how a book or story made them feel ("Learning Style Differences"). Girls are good at expressing their feelings, perhaps because both thinking and feeling abilities are located in the same area of the brain (Davila).

The usual, coed classroom isn't working for boys. "From kindergarten on, the education system rewards self-control, obedience, and concentration—qualities that … are much more common among girls than boys …Boys fidget, fool around, fight, and worse." As a consequence, boys have been "medicalized," and if that didn't work, they were sent to special education, often misused as a place to put "problem kids." Boys seldom go on to college, after spending their school time in special education classes, the surest way to a middle-class lifestyle (Poe).

The first thing you'd notice in a classroom designed for boys, is the noise. It's LOUD. (Remember, the hearing of boys is not as keen as that of girls.) The chairs are hard, to keep the boys awake. There is lots of movement. The teacher is moving all the time; a boy doesn't know when he'll be called on. When asking a question, the teacher is advised to "Get in their face. Raise your voice. Stand right in front of your student, nose-to-nose" and make him prove his answer. Formally address him as "Mr.," with his last name, as a means of increasing class discipline. "If you treat boys like men, they are more likely to act like men." This type of confrontation will make him "work harder and be prepared."

And what might the teacher be teaching? If a literature class, for example, the subject is probably non-fiction, preferred by boys, and dealing with "the way things work": action. Boys also like to read about heroic male protagonists such as Aron Ralston, mountain climber, who had to cut off his own arm to survive, His book, Between a Rock and a Hard Place, details his life-threatening experience. Assignments, in all subjects, would be objective ("Learning Style Differences"). Sax advices teacher to stay clear of "feeling" questions when teaching boys—"It's the worst thing a teacher can do." He thinks the explanation is that boys have their ability to think and their ability to feel "in completely different parts of the brain" (Davila).

Some fear that separation will bring back gender stereotypes. Dr. Sax speaks to the fear of some, when he says that there is no plan to go back to home economics for girls and woodworking shop for boys. That kind of stereotyping is in the past and will stay there. A single-sex education of today would, instead, increase the educational opportunities for both sexes (Davila).

Students in single-sex schools, and to a lesser degree in single-sex classes, often choose subjects they wouldn't dare choose in a coed school. They are relatively free of the gender stereotyping that exists in coed schools. Girls will dare to excel in math, computers, science, and sports because they see other girls doing so. The computer "geek" is a girl, the class president is a girl, etc. Boys, too, benefit from more diverse role models in a single-sex school. Consequently, boys feel free to follow their own interests and talents in subjects regarded as non-manly, such as art, music, and drama. Historian Steven Millies writes the following about his experience in attending a single-sex high school:

> I began high school more shy than most adolescents
> … but I did take the enormous step of joining the speech
> team, and that opened a new world to me It led me to
> other activities, and eventually to writing a column for the
> school paper The capstone came during my senior year
> when I debated a fiery teacher about the Vietnam War in
> front of our history classes The event drew so much
> attention that other people wanted to attend … When I
> think back on the catalyst—joining the speech team—and
> I consider the fact that forensics in Illinois is dominated
> by girls, about 70/30, I cannot imagine that I would have
> joined the team in a coed school … it would have been a
> "girls' thing." Knowing the south side of Chicago as I do,
> I have to believe that any boy who joined the team would
> have been making himself a target I needed the chance to
> explore my own potential without worrying about looking
> foolish in front of the girls ("Advantages for Boys")

It isn't as if we'd be trying something new if we adopted

single-sex education. We have a history of single-sex education,

and we still have some single-schools today. A selective list of

women who have come out of women's colleges include

Madeline Albright, Julia Child, Hilary Rodham Clinton,

Katharine Hepburn, Brigadier General Elizabeth P. Hoisington,

Jeanne Kirkpatrick, Margaret Mitchell, Nancy Pelosi, Nancy

Reagan, Diane Sawyer, Meryl Streep, Gloria Steinem, and Alice

Walker. In addition, graduates of women's colleges are paid

higher salaries than are women graduates of coeducational

colleges. Part of the reason for this could be the fact that there are more women graduating with math and science degrees from women's colleges than from coed colleges.

An article in the Arizona Daily Star (August 25, 2004), "More Public Schools Prefer 'His' and 'Hers'," informs us that "John Kerry, George W. Bush, his father, and Al Gore all went to all-boys schools" (Austin).

Conclusion

With so many proven advantages of single-sex education over coeducation, why do we persist in teaching the sexes in the same way? We seem to feel that "same" means equality of opportunity, but it doesn't. In this case "same" cheats both sexes. Girls and boys aren't the same, and we need to teach to their strengths—their differences.

For their own good, let's give Reuben and Rachel some of they want: separation from each other. In a single-sex classroom, each sex will have the best hope of learning and of realizing potential gifts.

Essay 7—Techno-Crazy

> There's a big lie coming down the pipe. It's the big
> lie of the educational technologist. Buy this educational
> software! Buy this multimedia system! Wire up your
> classroom because this educational software will (here
> comes the lie), make learning fun. It's a lie! It's a fraud!
>
> --Clifford Stoll[28]

Our modern society does have its benefits, such as labor saving devices of all kinds to make our lives physically easier. No one would exchange a tractor for a team of horses, or a modern washer/dryer for a washboard. With the telephone, and the cell phone, it is very easy to "reach out and touch someone"; this is wonderful in emergencies, and useful to keep in touch socially. Computers, with their ease and speed of computation, have greatly advanced our scientific knowledge. Our personal computers let us search libraries all over the world, and with e-mail we can quickly and easily contact anyone, almost any place in the world. Oh, and let's not forget all the games we can play! In addition to our computers for information and entertainment, we have television, with its multitude of channels. We now have so many "toys" to help and amuse us that we have no time to consider what these toys have cost us. The costs vary from mild to severe

Many of our labor saving devices are relatively harmless. They save us time and effort. In the time saved, we can do other things, such as going to the gym to work off the extra calories we've put on now that we have labor saving devices

Technology that does harm to our physical, mental, and emotional life, however, is a serious matter. Cell phones, personal computers, and television, all sing a siren song, promising much, but failing to mention side effects (just as do the commercials we are subjected to on all of these devices). The side effects are especially harmful for children whose brains are not yet fully developed. In fact, technology is turning our children into programmed robots, lacking imagination and the ability to think critically; our children are "damaged goods."

Let's take a closer look at the three main technological culprits: cell phones, computers, and television.

Cell phones are so convenient and in case of an emergency—one may save your life. On the other hand, we can almost always be reached, whether it is convenient or not—it's hard to escape! With cell phones, we are all at each other's "beck and call." A Psychology Today article, "A Nation of Wimps," refers to the cell phone as "the eternal umbilicus." Children can't get away from their parents; hence, they don't mature as they should. Where before they had to use their brains to plan meetings with their friends, for example, now they just flip open their cell phone and say, "Meet me at the library in five minutes." Things can be done so quickly—just get out that cell phone—that they don't learn how to be patient. They have trouble dealing with life's frustrations. This does not bode well for lasting relationships (Marano 64).

Surprisingly, the convenience of the cell phone may lead to depression. The planning part of our brain, our "executive branch," is in the prefrontal cortex (PFC) The PFC is "deeply implicated in depression," states Marano. Our PFC "feels good" when we set goals and work toward them, doing this on an everyday basis can actually build up a resistance to depression. But if our PFC doesn't get this kind of intellectual challenge, depression can move in and stay ("Nation of Wimps," 66). Later in this essay, I will cite statistics that link television watching to the high rate of teen suicide, but if everyday cell phone use leads to depression; it, too, may be a teen suicide risk.

Before we leave the subject of cell phones and go on to personal computers, we need to spotlight a new crime that involves both of them: bullying. "One in four 11- to 19-year-olds in the UK has been bullied or threatened through their mobile phone or PC," reports a National Children's Home (NCH) study.[29] Of those surveyed, 29 percent said that they had told no one—if bullied by phone, they may fear it would be taken from them. Bullying comes in more than one form: text bullying may be messages that are threatening or uncomfortable; camera phones and personal computers bully by sending pictures that make the recipient feel "threatened, embarrassed or uncomfortable." They also may feel trapped, for the bullies seem always able to reach them. A child's cell phone is a "treasured personal possession" that is seldom turned off—almost always available, the victim of cell-phone bullying may feel hopelessly trapped ("Cell Phone Bullying")

If you're not being bullied, personal computers are such fun! If you're bored, there are games to play, but that can get you into big trouble, warns Matt Bachl. Writing in the Sun-Herald of 15 October 2006, he relates the cost Michael Aspinall, age thirty-four, of Melbourne, Australia, paid for his addiction to computer gaming. Computer game playing in Australia is not unusual—53 percent of his countrymen (13 percent more than Europeans), play regularly. Michael, however, played more often than most.

> For ten years, he would play for eight hours a day and said if he didn't get his "fix," he'd be anxious and irritable.

"I used to take caffeine tablets to stay awake to play," he said. "Then I would smoke marijuana to come down off the high the game gave me."

Mr. Aspinall said his marriage broke up over his addiction and he lost his job because he was always tired. When he was unemployed, he locked himself in his room and played 20 hours a day.

"In the games you can be somebody you're not…you live a life you would like to lead," he said.

Mr. Aspinall spent tens of thousands of dollars upgrading hardware, internet speeds and buying games.

"It's not just the money you lose, but your life. You become out of touch with society altogether."

Bachl reports that Michael is in treatment for his addiction, but this is definitely not an Australian problem alone. The Clinic in Amsterdam is swamped with calls, and in the US, the Computer Addiction Study Center in Massachusetts is "treating dozens of addicts." South Koreans are obsessed with gaming, and experts consider it a bigger addiction than gambling, alcohol, or drugs (Bachl).

If you need information, visit an online library from your home computer; it's so convenient. Searching the web, however, may get you to people and places you'd rather not encounter, such as the legion of web pornographic sites that sometimes even sneak into serious search sites. So if you have a library not very far away, visit it. You may find even better sources of information on a shelf there—you wouldn't be able to see that shelf online. You'll also find like-minded people at the library to talk with; maybe you'll make a friend for life.

E-mail would be hard to give up; it's such a quick way to take care of the obligation to write to friends. But if you've ever had loads of unwanted spam and a virus or two, writing a letter and sending it by "snail mail," doesn't seem so arduous after all. Your recipient would value it more—it might even be saved and someday be part of a published memoir.

Newspapers, though it's predicted that they may in time go the way of the manual typewriter, can give you the news of the world and of Wall Street, crossword puzzles, and the daily horoscope, and if you want to save something, cut it out! No need to use your paper and printer ink.

Internet pioneer, Clifford Stoll, now believes that computers in the classroom are mostly a waste; they are addicting and harmful. In high school, he had fun playing with computers, he said, but he learned none of the astronomy skills he needed from the computer: "In fact, the more time I spend using a computer, the more time I'm online, the more I dull those very skills." He admits that some things can be learned via computer:

1. We can learn "factoids."

2. We learn to accept what the machine says without argument.

3. We learn that web page, chat room, and E-mail relationships are fleeting and shallow.

4. We learn to deal with frustration by unplugging and rebooting.

Stoll's most valuable high school class was English; where he learned to write, argue, speak publicly, and put arguments together. His advice to young people: take tough classes—not the computer (Interview by Aline McKenzie).

Dr. Joseph Chilton Pearce believes children should not use computers until they are at least twelve years old. Children need to learn how to think, to be able to understand abstractions, metaphors, and symbolism before they use the computer (quoted in "Expressing Life's Wisdom").

Television is ubiquitous. According to the recent statistics (2008), 99 percent of Americans own television sets, and the average family owns 2.83 sets ("The Effects of Television"). Watching television together can be a sharing time for a family, and it can be a springboard for reading more about what caught your interest while viewing. Great television can teach important life lessons. Sensitive issues depicted on television can make it easier for parents and children to discuss them later, with the television turned off to show proper attention and respect between the discussants. Cultural programs can open up the world of music and art for old and young. News and current events and documentaries can get young people, all people, thinking about the world and social issues. At its beginning, television was envisioned as becoming a great learning device. Too often, however, it falls far short of that.

Television creates a mesmerizing virtual world that may cause watchers to lose touch with their surroundings. The programs too often are frivolous, outlandish, and trivial. It entertains us, but it also abuses us.[30] Especially numerous are commercials; they have made us the ultimate consumers by "locking" into lower order behaviors, " the drives for food, territory, and sexuality...all to keep the wheels of industry turning" (*Evolution's End*, 200). A commercial will extoll the wonders of a new prescription drug, but gloss over the side effects; so too with the drug called "television," which can have serious side effects on our children, damaging them physically, emotionally, and mentally.

Physical Damage

Obesity is on the rise among children, and watching television for too many hours a day is a major reason. They don't get the exercise they should, and it presents them with ads encouraging the consumption of high fat and sugar foods. According to Dr. Norman Herr of California State University at Northridge, in four hours of watching Saturday morning cartoons, a child is exposed to 200 junk food ads. Multiply that by the number of Saturdays in a year, and the total will blow you away.

A diet high in fat and sugar can be life threatening later, leading to "heart disease, diabetes, high blood pressure, cancer, early puberty, liver disease, respiratory problems, sleep problems and a host of other disorders." It also increases the rate of adult mortality—earlier death ("The Effects of Television"). In the United States, "Obesity is lowest among children watching one or fewer hours of television a day, and highest among those watching four or more hours of television a day." Girls, being less physically active in general, are more at risk than boys. For both boys and girls, sedentary behaviors must give way to a more active lifestyle if we hope to halt the increase of obesity (Archives). The younger the child is, the greater the risk.

University of Glasgow and Bristol researchers report that "three-year-old children who watch more than eight hours of TV a week, are at a higher risk of obesity," They admit that genetics may be a factor in some cases, but usually the environment is the main culprit. Obesity has doubled "among two to four-year-olds since the early 1990s, while the rate has trebled for six- to fifteen-year-olds," says Dr. Ian Campbell, president of the National Obesity Forum. "[Parents] must stop them [from] watching TV and playing computer games all the time—these lifestyle factors are key" (quoted in "TV 'Increases Child Obesity Risk'").

Dimitri Christakis, associate professor of pediatrics at the University of Washington and Children's Hospital in Seattle, noticed how "enchanted" his three-month old son was with television, and it got him to wondering what this might be doing to his son's mind. With his colleagues, he designed a study to find out. The study included 1,345 children, whose parents were asked how much TV their children had watched at the ages of one, and three, and how well the children were able to pay attention at the age of seven. (To determine attention ability, the parents answered questions based on those from a hyperactivity behavioral profile.) "Christakis discovered that with each additional hour of television a child watched a day before age four, a child's risk of having attention problems at age seven increased by 9 percent" (Aimee Cunningham). Dr. Herr states that "children under three should not watch TV at all." He goes on to accuse TV of becoming a virtual babysitter, and says, "It is not a coincidence that…Attention Deficit Disorder (ADD) and Attention Deficit Hyperactive Disorder (ADHD) are prevalent…"

Television has become a status symbol in our society, and it does have benefits. Limited television watching of such shows as Sesame Street, Arthur, and Nova, can be a learning experience for children over the age of three. Even better is shared TV watching, making it a beneficial family time. All television watching should be monitored by parents, with limits set as to when children can, and when they cannot, watch TV. Avoid violent or sexually explicit programming, and Dr. Herr advises parents to "adhere as much as possible to the viewing time limit of 2-3 hours a day. He adds that children should not have television sets in their bedrooms. "Children are a blessing and parents—their life givers and protectors—must control what is in their environment."

Emotional Damage

Television ads do more than just promote fattening food; they also bombard viewers with ads that can affect a child's self-esteem, either consciously or through subliminal brainwashing—little things in ads that we don't consciously notice, but which can influence us because our brain has picked up on them. It's all about creating desire for a product. Children have trouble separating needs from wants, and parents, seeking to please their children, give in and buy trendy items that their children want but don't need. Further, these items may not be appropriate.

A child is harmed emotionally when television is used as a shield, a "buffer," between the child and reality. We live in a dangerous world. While watching television, children are safe from physical harm and we know where they are, but buffering a child from real life experiences, some unpleasant, is denying the child the opportunity to mature, to learn coping skills.[31] By Catering to our children and "sanitizing" their childhood, they are becoming "a nation of wimps," according to Marano.

It is ironic that we seek to "buffer" our children from unpleasant life experiences, yet we allow them to watch violent television shows, depicting scenes of murder, rape, and all manner of unpleasantness. Enough exposure to such shows, and they may become "desensitized," and have less sympathy and empathy for others "Mindless viewing can idle the part of the brain that needs to make critical connections for healthy moral and social development" ("Brain Development"). Children are great imitators; if they see violent, aggressive behavior, and if they've seen enough of it to become desensitized, it is only logical that they may act it out.

Psychologists L. Rowell Huesmann, Leonard Eron, and others found that children who watched many hours of violence on television when they were in elementary school, tended to be more aggressive as teenagers. By keeping track of these youngsters into adulthood, Drs. Huesmann and Eron found that eight-year-old watchers of violence were now more apt to be arrested and prosecuted for criminal acts as adults. "...being aggressive as a child did not predict watching more violent TV as a teenager, suggesting that TV watching may more often be a cause rather than a consequence of aggressive behavior" ("The Effects of Television").

Recent acts of violence by youth--Columbine, Virginia Tech—were preceded by hours of playing violent video and computer games or watching violent movies. They see violence as an acceptable way of solving problems ("The Effects of Television"). As early as 1963, writes Pearce, studies have shown "a direct one-for-one correspondence between the content of television and behavior." He continues, "Violence on television produces violent behavior in young people. ... Life is shown to be expendable and cheap, yet we condemn them for acting violently (*Evolution's End*, 169-70).

Before leaving grade school, the average child has seen 200 murders a year. By the age of eighteen, the number is a total of

175

200,000! Another alarming statistic is the suicide rate of young people. It's gone up 300 percent since 1950, the year people really began watching TV, and in the years that followed, the suicide rate grew as the number of TV's in homes grew (Dr. Herr). I'd say this was more than coincidental.

Daycare children show behavior problems that correspond to the amount of time they spend in day care. "About 26 percent of children who spend more than 45 hours per week in day care go on to have serious behavior problems at kindergarten age" (Lang). The problems may start before kindergarten, and television watching may very well be part of the problem. Many daycare children are routinely set down in front of a television screen. Could day care television watching be part of the reason for the necessity of preschools to expel 5,000 children each year? The children expelled were from state-funded pre-kindergarten programs ("Preschools Expel"). A study from researchers at the University of Washington found that the more television watched by four-year-olds, the more likely are they to become bullies in elementary school: "Every hour parked in front of the television increases the odds of bullying by nine percent" (quoted in "TV Time Linked").

On the subject of violent "entertainment," Dr. Alice Miller says, "Children who have really been loved and protected will not be interested in these films and shows and will not be in danger" (quoted in *Roots*). Put another way, she is saying that if children are interested in these shows (and films), they should NOT watch them. What they really need is more love and security to the extent that they are no longer interested in violent "entertainment."

No matter how you look at it, violent shows should be forbidden—they're either boring or dangerous-- the best thing is not to let children watch them A busy mother should think twice before plunking her child down in front of the television to watch violence. If bored, the show is not going to keep the child occupied anyway, and if the child is not bored, it may be a sign that the violence is doing some dangerous things to the psyche. Plunk him down with some colored play dough instead. It will exercise his imagination.

A psyche showing signs of damage in preschool and kindergarten is probably a foreshadowing of what's to come. Anxieties, depression, and lack of self-control during the formative years can pursue a person for life. According to Marano, if children have "few challenges all their own, kids are unable to forge their creative adaptations to the normal vicissitudes of life That not only makes them risk-averse, it makes them psychologically fragile, riddled with anxiety" ("A Nation of Wimps," 61).

The anxiety will follow them to college. The seriousness of mental health problems among students has been increasing since 1988. Anxiety affects an estimated 15 percent of college students and is the top mental health concern, edging our relationship problems (Though anxiety tops other mental health problems on college campuses, "obsessive pursuit," or "stalking," has increased in number and severity of incidents, and anorexia and bulimia affect forty percent of women at some time in their college career.) In an effort to deal with anxiety, students have increasingly turned to binge drinking and self-harming (Marano, "A Nation of Wimps" 62-64). "Self-harming" can extend all the way to suicide. As said above, "The youth suicide rate has increased about 300 % since 1950" (Dr. Herr).

After enough complaints by parents concerned about the grades their fragile students were earning, grades became inflated in colleges around the nation. Social historian Peter Stearns of George Mason University sees this as an "index of emotional overinvestment in a child's success" (quoted in Marano, "A Nation of Wimps," 62)

In spite of parents' efforts to protect their children and to promote their college success, reports from 90 percent of college counseling centers, show an increase in serious mental health problems. Colleges and universities, faced with having to balance the needs of these troubled students with the need to provide a safe learning environment, have resorted to forcing troubled students to drop out. The "force-outs" are triggered by the schools' fears of lawsuits (Feirman)

Mental Damage

Television commercials may be irritating, as may be many of the programs; but, according to Pearce, the effect of content is minor. Television has damaged us by replacing the storyteller in our homes.[32] The art of personal story telling and conversation have virtually died out. Parents no longer play with their children as they once did, they are too busy watching the "boob tube." Not only do our relationships suffer, but also the development of our children's minds and hearts. We are not there for each other as we once were. People no longer visit each other as they once did. What happened to Bridge Games? And doubling over with laughter at the person acting out a title in Charades?

"The major damage of television ... is neurological and it has, indeed, damaged us perhaps beyond repair." The infant's brain is "flooded" with images at the very time when the brain is supposed to make its own images Television short-circuits the process by providing not only the stimulus [for image making] but also the response [the image] (*Evolution's End*, 164) As Pearce put it:

> Television floods the brain with a counterfeit of the response the brain is supposed to learn to make to the stimuli of words or music As a result, much structural coupling between mind and environment is eliminated; few metaphoric images develop; few higher cortical areas of the brain are called into play; few, if any, symbolic structures develop (*Evolution's End*, 166)

The child's failure to develop the ability to "image within" means that the power to imagine does not develop—most of the brain is unemployed. If children "can't 'see what the mathematical symbol or the semantic words mean; nor the chemical formulae; nor the concept of civilization as we know it,' they are bored. "They can't comprehend the subtleties of our Constitution or Bill of Rights..." Such abstractions hold no interest for them because they simply can't "get it." Only physical stimulus grabs their interest, and they become restless if it is not forthcoming (Pearce, *Evolution's End*, 167).

If children can't imagine, they can't learn and can't hope: that is tragic. They become victims of the environment, because they can't "imagine" a different world Children who lack imagination are more apt to be violent, for they can't escape by way of imagining alternative behavior (*Evolution's End*, 168).

Pearce is not alone. An article put out by the University of California Cooperative Extension, titled "Brain Development and Impact of Television," stresses the importance of the years from birth to five. These are the years of early wiring of the brain, critical to a child's development. Too much TV viewing interferes with the child's opportunities to make brain connections. The TV produces alpha brain waves that create a trance state, allowing information to enter, but not allowing it to be processed or analyzed. Ever wonder why so many seem to "nod off" while watching TV? Now you know.

Eye development is also affected, for eyes do not move as much while watching TV, and thus are less stimulated. Ability to read suffers if children do not develop "rhythmical and controlled" eye movements. Even speech and language can be impacted: "Language development requires listening, interaction, and speaking." Television requires only hearing. Excessive amounts of TV can result in a lack of verbal language skills, and a more poorly wired brain due to less stimulation ("Brain Development").

Wiring of the brain can indeed be affected by television, and not necessarily by watching programs By just being in the same room while adults are watching television, the rapidly growing brains of children aged one to three can be adversely affected. It may not be the content, but the medium itself that is doing the damage. A study of 2,600 children, aged one to three, begun in 1980, has led to the conclusion that the more television this age group watched, the more apt they would be to suffer from "attention span deficit " by age seven (Fields). [Just what the aforementioned Christakis study showed.]

In the last thirty years, there has been an explosion in the number of children diagnosed with attention disorders. Genetics and drugs are usually given as the cause, but now critics are beginning to wonder if our environment might also be a reason. After all, television has been cited as a factor in child obesity and violence, could it be that there is something in the very nature of the television image itself that may be at least partly to blame? (Fields).

Is it any wonder that in our age of the ever-present TV— present even in children's bedrooms, and 66 percent of us watch television at dinner—teachers are having trouble with unruly students and that students are having trouble learning?

Neural damage to our children from television has made around 70 percent of our children incapable of learning. Pearce: "The 30 percent or so of our children still capable of learning in school have been read to and played with by their parents, generally in addition to television and mountains of plastic junk This shows how little attention is needed to nourish the brain and get its creativity going" (*Evolution's End*, 169).

Yes, he said "plastic junk," meaning toys. We give our children so many toys! We inundate them "with objects that don't stand for something but already are." No need any longer to create toys—to use the imagination. The days of clothespin or "corn" dolls, of cars and trucks made from old roller skates, and of cardboard castles--gone forever. What a shame! When children had to fashion their own toys, they were creative and imaginative and so were the games they played with them. Imagination is the key to learning, to achievement. Child's play is the real antidote to television; it is social and it is fun. Child's play is the road to becoming a successful adult.

Next to keeping our children safe, we want them to be "successful" adults The American family concentrates so hard on making each member a "success," that it often produces mental illness in each of its members:

> Each individual is gradually converted into a device with a built-in design for achievement in accordance with the prevailing requirements, entailing the suppression of emotion, the denial of love and friendship, the ability to trade with whatever serves one for a conscience, while conveying an unvarying appearance of rectitude (Montagu, 315)

In addition to parents' trying to take all discomfort and disappointment out of their children's lives, they are now trying to remove playtime as well Children used to have recess, but many schools no longer do. Play has become commercialized. Adults manage organized sports, and children don't have to learn how to settle disputes, the adult referee does it for them Marano writes:

> Play helps children learn how to control themselves, how to interact with others... it's in play that cognitive agility really develops. Studies of children and adults around the world demonstrate that social engagement actually improves intellectual skills. It fosters decision-making, memory and thinking, speed of mental processing ("A Nation of Wimps" 64)

"Play," states Pearce, "is the very force of society and civilization, and a breakdown in ability to play will reflect in a breakdown of society." It not only develops our brain's abilities, but it helps us to become more effective future parents (*Evolution's End*, 164).

For too many of today's children, every minute is carefully scheduled—there's virtually no "free time" to play—no time to develop the imagination. Parents are so bent on their children's success, both academically and socially, that they dominate their children's lives and allow the children to dominate theirs. They drive them to sports practices, ballet lessons, and what have you.

Verrengia writes about such non-stop activity in his article, "Modern American Family." He focuses on Jake Zeiss, who dashes from his west Los Angeles home before 8 o'clock in the morning, with "red hair damp and shirttail flapping":

> He's in for a hectic day, as usual. After seven hours of back-to-back meetings, he still has enough energy to volley tennis balls with a pro. Then it's into his Mercedes where he "snarfs" down a nutritious bar and settles down to do his paperwork on a lapdesk as his chauffeur snakes through rush hour traffic. Jake Zeiss is only nine years old, and his paperwork is arithmetic. As he searches for a pencil, he comes across a yo-yo and is sorely tempted. His mother, Kim, the chauffeur, quickly quashes that idea by loudly asking him if he thinks that's a good use of his time, followed by, "How many problems have you done?"
>
> They're late for hockey practice. After that it's a fencing lesson at the gym for Jake's ten-year-old sister, Madison. The family hopes to meet up at the gym when

their father, Gary, arrives—it's hoped—by 8 p.m. (Verrengia).

This strained, too busy, two paycheck family has little time for each other. Though they do eat dinner together, at 10:20 p.m. when Madison returns home after fencing practice. After so many hours on the go, they are just all played out

Researchers contend that a family such as this is setting itself up to "erode from within." They are damaging their children by not allowing them time to play. No time exists for playful interaction, no time for conversation, courtesy, or intimacy. Such busyness is by design: Kim and Gary believe it's a "key to being a successful adult in a culture that rewards "multi-taskers" (quoted by Verrengia). The only good thing about being so busy is that they have no time for television.

Yet, Kim and Gary's dreams may not be realized. Their children may go off to college, lacking decision-making skills, interpersonal relationship skills, and just plain coping skills. They won't know how to act when free of parental hovering. They'll be sitting ducks for anxiety and other psychological problems. Perhaps they'll be sent home because their problems are too many or too serious. Their parents would be devastated/

Lacking any common interests of their own because of their narrow focus on their children, this disappointment will probably lead to divorce. Could their fragile, anxious children take the blow? Kim and Gary may find out too late that the "key to being a successful adult" is not in becoming a multi-tasker. The road to success may actually be child's play "True play," says Pearce," is the ability to play with one's reality. Thus, imagination gives resiliency, flexibility, endurance, and the capacity to forego immediate reward on behalf of long-term strategies" (*Evolution's End*, 168). Play does much to turn a child into a mature, independent adult. Isn't that what parenting is all about?

Conclusion

Technology may be the ruin of us; perhaps it already is. Pearce refers to today's children as "damaged goods" in his book, *Evolution's End* (170). The damage is physical, emotional, and mental, and is perpetrated by our so-called "technological marvels"—cell phones, computers, and television.

Cell phones and computers open our children's privacy to invaders that can exploit and manipulate them. Cell phones also encourage dependency, "the eternal umbilicus," according to Marano.

By far, television does the most damage: it interferes with play, a part of a child's preparation for adulthood; it encourages obesity; and watching violence may lead to violent behavior in the susceptible. Most damaging of all, the wiring of the brains of the very young can be permanently affected, interfering with their ability to imagine. The child who can't imagine can't learn

"Imagination is more Important than Knowledge."
--Albert Einstein: *On Science*

Footnotes

[1] We can only speculate on how women knew they needed iron-rich meat. They may have noticed that they felt better when they ate meat. Shlain chalks it up to Intuition and native intelligence (41).

[2] "Myelination" is a process by which a layer of fat coats wiry fibers connecting regions of the brain. This makes the brain's actions more precise and efficient. This process begins at birth and takes around twenty years to complete.

[3] People with access to computers are usually not poor. Pornography and obsession with sex is a by-product of affluence (Morgan 227-229).

[4] A large Australian study (2001): "Both boys and girls who were educated in single-sex classrooms scored on average 15 to 22 percentile ranks higher than did boys and girls in coeducational settings" (quoted "Single-Sex vs. Coed").

[5] "The original Typhoid Mary was a New York City cook in the early 1900s who loved her job. Unfortunately, she had been exposed to typhoid, and although she was immune to the disease herself, she was able to pass the disease to others by way of the food she prepared. Health officials identified her as Mary Mallon, an Irish-born immigrant, and they quarantined her to stop the spread of the disease. Three years later, Mary was released with a warning not to cook professionally again. But in 1915, she was discovered working as a cook at a maternity hospital identified as the source of a new typhoid outbreak, and she was forcibly returned to quarantine, where she remained until her death in 1938." (quoted from "The Word of the Day." <word@m-w.com>14 Jan. 2005)

[6] Evolution going backwards

[7] Maureen Dowd's mother felt that Martha Stewart was "railroaded" by "jealous men." Dowd, quoting her mother, continues: "If men could figure out how to have babies, they'd get rid of us altogether." If Dowd's mother is right, men feel more than jealousy; they feel rage ("TV Still").

[8] Jane Goodall writes about war between rival groups of chimpanzees in her book, *Through a Window.* She found that patrolling males would almost always badly injure, even kill, stranger females (98-111). As we humans share 98.4 percent of our DNA with chimpanzees, perhaps we come by this bad behavior genetically, but that does not mean that we have to continue it.

Goodall also tells of occasions of cannibalism among the chimpanzees, behavior considered an intolerable aberration in humans.

[9] Robb's "licensed companions" are independent professionals, selling their sexual favors. At the age of eighteen or above, a person choosing to become a licensed companion applies for a license, acquires a place in which to do business, furnishes it, and agrees to regular health check-ups. Licensed companions are not allowed to use drugs. They pay taxes like any other small business, and they are protected by the law, rather than prosecuted. They are not under the thumb of any pimp. In Robb's futuristic world, rapes were reduced in number, but not eliminated; rape is usually about control, not sex.

[10] In the event that a licensed companion encounters a client that refuses to wear a condom, there is now a vaginal "gel" being tested that, it is hoped, will prevent HIV from invading vaginal tissue. It has proved to be a "potent protector" of female monkeys who were exposed to large amounts of the AIDS virus ("Gel Shows Promise"). This gel, if it tests well, could also prove to be a lifesaver to wives of husbands who have extramarital sexual encounters.

[11] Banerjee reported that "many Indian men who visit prostitutes are reluctant to wear condoms, which they say reduce sexual pleasure" (quoted in "Prostitutes' Rights").

[12] According to Montagu, "The need to be touched is more basic than the need for sex." Only a few members of a species need to satisfy sexual tension in order for a species to survive, but touching, skin-to-skin stimulation, is a "universal need." It is necessary to the behavioral health of every individual;" Tactile deprivation in infancy usually results in behavioral inadequacies in later life" (318).

[13] Direct-entry midwives (DEMs) are self-employed entrepreneurs. They enter midwifery education directly, without becoming nurses first. In the United States, direct-entry midwives are "legal, regulated, and licensed, registered, or certified in fourteen states." Direct-entry midwives are the norm in Europe, where would-be midwives commonly attend formal three-year midwifery training programs in post-secondary educational programs or universities (Davis-Floyd).

[14] Montagu, 190; Pearce, *Evolution's* 112.

[15] Pearce writes, "… the mother often experiences her reaction to this abandonment as 'postpartum blues,' a depression considered a medical

enigma; she, too, is cut off from the bonding that was supposed to happen"(124).

[16] Sources: International Childbirth Education Association, P.O. Box 20048, Minneapolis, MN 55420; American Foundation for Maternal and Child Health, 439 E. 51 Street, New York, NY 10022; NAPSAC International, Box 646, Marble Hill, MO 63764.

[17] Midwifery, with the proper licensure, is legal in the following states: Alaska, Arkansas, Arizona, California, Colorado, Florida, Louisiana, Montana, New Hampshire, New Mexico, Oregon, South Carolina, Texas, and Washington. It is illegal in nine states and the District of Columbia (Davis-Floyd).

[18] Pearce credits the addition of hormones to animal feed, and the subsequent ingestion of food products from these animals to be to blame for "an immediate unprecedented explosion in the growth patterns of an entire generation: and "strangely coincident" with the proliferation of child sexual abuse (*Evolution's End,* 198-100).

[19] Miller thinks 100 percent of inmates in American prisons have been abused as children (*Banished,* 27).

[20] Miller tells of a child born with three ulcers as the result of abuse in the womb. The mother was beaten during pregnancy and used drugs. The child died ("Roots").

[21] Marilyn Heins, M.D., owner of <www.parentkidsright.com> and author of ParenTips, Development Publications, 1999.

[22] From the *BBC* comes news of a plan to separate black boys from classmates to improve their school performance. The head of the Commission for Racial Equality has suggested that black fathers "not living with their sons should be denied access if they refused to attend parents' evenings"; he believes that lack of self-esteem and positive role models partly account for the poor school performance, as well as the attitude that good grades are not cool ("Black Boys").

[23] If possible, a mother should stay home until the children are in school, and many are choosing to spend more time at home with their children (Wallis). But women who are employed are healthier than those unemployed, provided they have no child under six at home (Noonan).

[24] In 2003, there were 8,076 pregnancies in girls under the age of sixteen in England and Wales ("Parents").

191

[25] "Myelination" is a process by which a layer of fat coats wirelike fibers connecting regions of the brainThe effect is to make the actions of the brain more precise and efficient

[26] From <u>BBC News</u>: The United Kingdom wants many more girls to earn IT-related degrees At present, women make up only one in five of the technology workforce The South East England Development Agency is funding a "scheme" designed to encourage 150,000 girls aged 10 to 14 to plan for IT careers ("Scheme").

[27] Researchers, Jean and Geoffrey Underwood, gave thirty-one pairs of eight-year-olds a computer based language taskThe pairs--girl-girl, girl-boy, or boy-boy-- were matched for reading abilityIt was found that putting a girl with a boy "degraded her performance by 50 percent" ("Advantages for Girls").

[28] Clifford Stoll, astronomer and computer expert, author of *The Cuckoo's Egg* and *Silicon Snake Oil*, is working on a new book "arguing against computers in schools."

[29]Bullying is also linked to time spent watching TV ("TV Time Linked".

[30] "Child abuse is defined as the emotional, physical or sexual neglect or maltreatment by others that can cause serious emotional, physical, cognitive or mental disorders. I am maintaining the negative effects of television on children are tantamount to child abuse....

....I am referring to the TV as the abuser. While not a person, the TB is both the device conveying the information, which causes the negative effects of television on children [and adults], and the symbol of the corporate person, that is to say, those who are involved in creating what emanates from the TV (Herr).

[31] Pearce sees irony in that we buffer children against danger during the formative years, and then at about age sixteen, "put [them] behind the wheel of two or three hundred horsepower, turn [them] loose on the freeways, and wonder why the vast majority of automobile accidents occur with young drivers" (*Exploring the Crack in the Cosmic Egg,* 99).

[32] Radio did the opposite; it sparked the imagination Some may remember the vivid images they saw in their heads while listening to "The Shadow," "The Lone Ranger," and just WHAT did Fibber McGee have in his closet?

Bibliography

ABRAMS, DOUGLAS CARLTON. "Father Nature: The Making of a Modern Dad."

Psychology Today. Mar./Apr. 2002: 38-47.

"ADVANTAGES FOR BOYS." *National Association for Single Sex Public Education. 27 Aug. 2004 <http://www.singlesexscdhools.org>*

"ADVANTAGES FOR GIRLS" *National Association for Single Sex Public Education.* 1 Aug. 2004 <http://www.singlesexschools.org/adgirls.html>

"AIDS OUT OF CONTROL IN INDIA." *CBS News* 15 Apr. 2004 <http://www.cbsnews.com/stories/2004/04/08/60minutes/printable610961.shtml

"AMERICANS FOR DIVORCE." *Divorce Reform.* 20 Dec. 2004<http://www.divorceform.org/www.divorcereform.org/lea.html>

"ARAB MILITIAS RAPING, KILLING FEMALES OF ALL AGES IN SUDAN." *Arizona Daily Star.* 20 July 2004: A8.

ARCHIVES OF PEDIATRICS AND ADOLESCENT MEDICINE, Mar. 2001. 9 June 2005 http://archpedi.ama-assn.org/cgi/content/abstract/155/3/360

ARMOUR, STEPHANIE. "More Men Seek Better Work-Life Balance." *USA Today* 8 Oct. 2003: B5.

AUSTIN, LIZ. "More Public Schools Prefer 'His' and 'Hers.'" *Arizona Daily Star* 25 Aug. 2004: A16.

AXTMAN, KRIS. "Judicial Rarity: Death Penalty in a Rape Case." *Christian Science*

Monitor. 15 Oct. 2003
<http://www.scmonitor.com/2003/0908/p02s02- usju.htm>

BACHL, MATT. "Computers Breed New Addiction." 12 Aug.
1995. 7 Aug. 201<http://www.the
age.com.au/news/games/computers-breed-new-addiction/>

BALES, KEVIN. "How We Can End Slavery." *National
Geographic.* 9 Oct. 2003

http://magma.national.com/ngn/0309/feature1/online_extra.html>

BARUA, MANOSHI. "Victims of Acid Attacks." *BBC News.* 22
Dec. 2003

<http://www.bbc.co.uk/worldservice/people/features/ihavearightt
o/four_b/report-barua.shtml>

BLACKBURN, HEATHER A., and STACEY M.
THOMAS. *Rape Warfare.* 12 Apr.
2004<http://jrscience.wep.muchio.edu/Research/HnatureProposal
sArticles/RapeWarfare.html>

BLAKE, WILLIAM. "The Clod & the Pebble." *The Norton
Anthology of English*

Literature. (Rev. Vol. 2). Ed. M.H. Abrams, et al. New York:
Norton, 1968.

BOWER, BRUCE. "The Ties That Bond." *Science News* 9 Aug.
1997: 94-5.

BOWMAN, LEE. "Teen Brains Found to Develop Judgment
Slowly." *Arizona Daily Star* 18 May 2004: A4.

BOYD, ROBERTS. "Mate Poachers, Poachees Rife in
Romance's Jungle." *Arizona Daily Star* 16 Nov. 2003: A8.

"BRAIN DEVELOPMENT AND IMPACT OF TELEVISION."
Developed by Sharon K. Junge.*University of California
Corporation Extension.* 15 June 2005

<http://ucce.ucdavis.edu/files/filelibrary/1808/14213.pdf>

"BREAST MILK LOWERS BLOOD PRESSURE." *BBC News*. 24 May 2005
<http://news.bbc.co.uk/1/hi/health/4572185.stm>

"BREASTFEEDING AND COMPLEMENTARY FEEDING." *Unicef Statistics.* 22 Apr. 2005<http://www.childinfo.org/eddb/brfeed/index.htm>

BURTON, ROBERT. "Lust." *Dictionary of Quotations.* Compiled by Bergen Evans.New York: Wings, 1969.

"CALL FOR MORE HELP ON HOME BIRTHS." *BBC News*. 23 Nov. 2004

<http://news.bbc.co.uk/1/hi/health/4033051.stm>

CALLANDER, MERYN G. "Myth: Hospital Births Are Safer Than Home Births."The Wellspring. 25 Apr. 2995 <http://www.thewellspring.com/TWO/5hospital_births.html>

"CAMERA CAPTURES BEATING OF BOY ON SCHOOL BUS." *WESH* 12 Feb. 2004. 25 May 2005 < http://wesh.com/print/2842076/detail.htm>

"CELL PHONE BULLYING." *P2p.net.* 2 June 2005 <http://p2pnet.net/story/5119>

CHESNICK, JOYESHA. "La Frontera Kids present Sex Dilemma." *Arizona Daily Star*

10 Apr. 2005: A1.

COCKBURN, ANDREW. "21st Century Slaves." *National Geographic* Sept. 2003:2-25.

"COMMITTEE TO DECRIMINALIZE PROSTITUTION: PROSTITUTION ACT OF 1996." 15 Oct. 2004<http://www.bayswan.org/decrim.html>

A COMPARISON OF THE U.S. TO OTHER RICH NATIONS. 2 June 2005
<http://<www.huppi.com/kangaroo/8Comparison.htm>

COOPERMAN, ALAN, and LENA H. SUN. "Hundreds of Priests Removed Since '60's."*Remnant of God.* 8 May 2004 <http://www.linearg.com/remnantofgod.molest69.htm>

"COVENANT MARRIAGE LINKS." *Divorce Reform.* 20 Dec. 2004

<http://www.divorcereform.org/cov.html>

CRIME. 18 May 2005 <http://www.crime.org/do/Home>

"CROWN OF THE PALACE." *Historical Significance.* 29 Dec. 2003

<http://rubens.anu.edu.au/student.projects/tajmahal/hist_sign.htm
l>

CRUICKSHANK, DOUGLAS. "Last Roundup at the Mustang Ranch." *Salon Rogues' Gallery.* 12 Dec. 2003
<http://www.salon.com/people/rogue/1999/08/12/mustang/print.h
tml>

CUNNINGHAM, AIMEE. "TV Weakens Attention." [Preview] 17 Nov. 2004. 05 Aug. 2012<http://www.scientificamerican.com/article.cfm?id=tv-weakens-attention>

DAVILA, VIANNA. "Expert Says Boys, Girls Learn Differently." *San AntonioExpress-News* 21 Jan. 2004. *National Association for Single Sex Public Education.* 9 Sept. 2004<http://www.genderdifferences.org/links-sanantonio.htm>

DAVIS-FLOYD, ROBBIE E. "The Ups and Downs of Direct-Entry Midwifery."1 May 2005 <http://www.davis-floyd.com/art_frame_neteduc13.html>

DEMPSTER, CAROLYN. "Rape Is Endemic in South Africa." *BBC News* 9 Apr. 2002.

28 Feb. 2004
<http://news.bbc.co.uk/1/hi/world/africa/1909220.stm>

"DESPITE PROGRESS, CHILDREN'S RIGHTS FAR FROM UNIVERSAL." Press release.*UNICEF.* 24 Nov. 2004
<http://www.unicef.org/media/media_24176.html>

DOWD, MAUREEN. 'Bush to World: Do as I Say, Not as I do." *Arizona Daily Star*

1 Mar. 2005: B5.

DOWLING, COLETTE. *The Frailty Myth: Women Approaching Physical Equality.*

New York: Random, 2000.

"THE EFFECTS OF TELEVISION." *Telewatcher. 05 Aug. 2012*
<http://telewatcher.com/telewatching/televisions-effect-on-children>

"11 FACTS ABOUT TEEN PREGNANCY." *Do Something.* 25 July 2012 <http://www.dosomething.org>

"FACTS ABOUT HUNGER." *Care Newsroom.* 10 Dec. 2003
<http://www.careusa.org/

newsroom/specialreports/hunger2003facts.asp>

FEIRMAN, JASON. "The New College Dropout." *Psychology Today.* May/June 2005: 38.

FIELDS, SUZANNE. "'Rewiring' the Brains of Children Through TV." *Arizona Daily Star* 17 Apr. 2004: B7.

FISHER, HELEN. "Biology." *Psychology Today.* 10 July w003 <http://

<www.psychologytoday.com/htdocs/prod/ptoarticle/pto-19930301-000030.asp>

---. *The First Sex: The Natural Talents of Women and How They Are*

CHANGING THE WORLD. New York: Random, 1999.

"GEL SHOWS PROMISE VS. HIV." *Arizona Daily Star* 15 Oct. 2004: A6.

"GENERAL FACTS AND STATS." *Teen Pregnancy.* 11 Nov. 2004 <http//

www.teenpregnancy.org/resources/data/genlfact.asp>

GILBOA, DAHLIA. "Mass Rape: War on Women." 15 Oct. 2003

<http://www.scrippscol.edu/~home/nrachlin/www/Dahlia.html>

GOLEMAN, DANIEL. *emotional intelligence.* new york: bantam, 1995.

GOODALL, JANE. *Through a Window.* Boston: Houghton, 1990.

HAMBLEN, STUART. "I Won't Go Huntin' with You Jack." *Digital Tradition Mirror.*

23 Dec. 2003 <http://sniff.numachi.com/~rickheit/dtrad/pages/tiWONTHUNT.html>

HARRISON, ANN. "Hookers Unite!" 25 Oct. 2004 <http://www.sfbg.com/38/18/cover_hookers.html>

HEINS, MARILYN. "Find Out if You Like Kids Before Having 'Em." *Arizona Daily Star* 22 May 2005: E8.

"HELEN OF TROY." *Microsoft Encarta Encyclopedia 2001.* CD-ROM. Microsoft

Corporation, 1993-2000.

HERR, NORMAN,Dr. "Negative Effects of Television Tantamount to Emotional Child Abuse in a Box." *Parenting Healthy Children 2007.* 05 Aug. 2012 <http://parenting-healthy-children.com/>

"HIV IN WOMEN RISING GLOBALLY, U. N. REPORTS." *Arizona Daily Star* 24 Nov.2004: A11.

"HOLMES REVEALS SELF-HARM ORDEAL." *BBC Sport.* 29 May 2005 <http://

news.bbc.co.uk/sport1/hi/athletics/4590655.stm>

"IN HARMS WAY: SUICIDE IN AMERICA." *National Institute of Mental Health* 2003.18 May 2005 <http://www.nimh.nih.gov/publicity/harmsway.cfm?Output=Print>

"INQUIRY EXAMINES SELF-HARM RATES." *BBC News.* 30 Mar 2004 <http://

news.bbc.co.uk/1/hi/health/3580365.stm>

JIRAPINYO, YUJIRA. "Prostitution in Thailand: What's the Solution?" *Siam Web*

Cyber Culture. 2 Jan. 2004 <http://www.siamweb.org/content/NewsCulture/155/index_eng.php>

KETTLEWELL, JULIANNA. "Fidelity Gene 'Found in Voles.'" *BBC News.* 17 June 2004

<http://news.bbc.co.uk/1/hi/sci/tech/3812483.stm>

KRAKOVSKY, MARINA. "Why One Kid May Be Enough." *Psychology Today.* Jan./

Feb. 2005: 31, 33.

KRISTOF, NICHOLAS E. "Atrocities Qualify as Genocide." *Arizona Daily Star*

17 June 2004: B7.

---. "In Darfur, Rape a Political Statement." *Arizona Daily Star* 12 June2005: H2.

LAMB, MICHAEL. "Hormones Vs. Culture." *Psychology Today.* Mar./Apr. 2002: 42.

LANG, HEIDE. "The Trouble with Day Care: Are Scientists Telling Parents the
Whole Truth?" *Psychology Today.* May/June 2005: 17-18.

"LEARNING STYLE DIFFERENCES." *National Association for Single Sex Public*

Education. 31 Aug. 2004
<http://www.singlesexschools.org/research-learning.htm>

LERMAN, DAVID. "Sexual Assaults Plague Military After Decades of Reform." *Business Week* 26 July 2012.
LOEWENBERG, SAMUAL. "Ana Patricia Botin." *Time* 20 Dec. 2004: 143.

LOST. Prod. J. J. Abrams and Damon Lindelof. ABC. KGUN. Tucson. 18 May 2005.

LOWER, RACHEL. "Elephants and Teenagers." *Article City.* 20 Nov. 2004

<http://www.articlecity.com/articles/parenting/article_86.shtml>

MARANO, HARA ESTROFF. "Here Comes Trouble." *Psychology Today.* Nov./

Dec. 2004:13-14.

---. "A Nation of Wimps." *Psychology Today.* Nov/Dec. 2004: 60-70, 103.

MARTINEZ, MARIANNE. "Report Finds Link Between Child Abuse and Crime."

AFRA News. 3 Dec. 2004. 4 June 2005
<http://<familyrightsassociation.com/news/archive/2004/dec/3.ht ml>

MEAD, MARGARET. 31 May 2004
<http://xplore.com/quotes/authors/m/margaret_mead.html>

MENDELSOHN, JENNIFER. "What We Know About Sex."
USA Weekend 7-9 Nov.

2003: 6-8.

MILLER, ALICE. *Banished Knowledge: Facing Childhood Injuries.* Trans. Leila

Vennewitz. New York: Doubleday, 1990.

---. "The Roots of Violence." Interview. By Diane Connors.
Omni Mar. 1987. 24 May 2005
<http://www.nospank.net/miller4.htm>

MONTAGU, ASHLEY. *Touching: The Human Significance of the Skin.* 2nd ed.

New York: Harper & Row, 1978.

MORGAN, ELAINE. *The Descent of Woman.* New York: Stein and Day, 1972.

MORTON, OLIVE M. "Parents' Early Choices Affect Children's Emotional Intelligence." *Learning Place Online.* 2 Mar. 2004
<http://

www.learningplaceonline.com/children/Morton/01-early-choices.htm>

"MOVE AIMS TO STOP HUMAN TRAFFICKING." *Arizona Daily Star* 5 Oct. 2004: A7.

NEILL, KEVIN GERARD, MPH. "Duty, Honor, Rape: Sexual Assault Against Women

During War." 21 Apr. 2004
<http://www.bridgew.edu/SoAS/jiws/nov00/duty.htm>

"NEV. BROTHEL OWNERS ASKING TO BE TAXED."
Arizona Daily Star 9 Apr. 2005. 30 Aug. 2005
<http://www.azstarnet.com/dailystar/news/69632.php>

NEWELL, L. ANNE. "Police: Abuse Led to Girl's Suicide."
Arizona Daily Star

7 May 2004: B1, 5.

NOONAN, PEGGY J. "Working Moms Are Healthier." *USA Weekend* 17-19 Sept.

2004:10-11.

"PARENTS 'MUST TACKLE TEEN BIRTH.'" *BBC News*. 26 May 2005 <http://

news.bbc.co.uk/1/hi/health/4581939.stm>
PARKER, KATHLEEN. "Presc[*sic*]ence of Father Is Best Thing for Daughter." *Divorce*

Reform. 16 Dec. 2004
<http://www.divorcereform.org/mel/afatherprescence.html>

PASSAR, DAWN. "Representing the Network of Sexwork Projects in Beijing 1995."
7 Jan. 2004 <http://www.bayswan.org/Dawn.html>
PAUL, PAMELA. "The Porn Factor." *Time* 19 Jan. 2004: 99-101.
PEARCE, JOSEPH CHILTON. *The Crack in the Cosmic Egg: Challenging Constructs of*

Mind & Reality. New York: Pocket Books, 1971.

---. *Evolution's End: Claiming the Potential of Our Intelligence.* San Francisco: Harper, 1992.

---. *Exploring the Crack in the Cosmic Egg: Split Minds & Meta-Realities.*

New York: Pocket, 1974.

---. "Expressing Life's Wisdom: Nurturing Heart-Brain Development Starting

with Infants." Interview by Chris Mercogliano and Kim Debus. *Journal*

of Family Life 5 (1999). 29 Feb 2004
<http://www.ratical.org/many-worlds/JCP.html>

"PENN STATE CHILD SEX ABUSE SCANDAL." 25 July 2012

"PRESCHOOLS EXPEL 5,000 KIDS ANNUALLY." *Arizona Daily Star* 17 May 2005: A3.

PRINCE-HUGHES, DAWN. *Gorillas Among Us: A Primate Ethnographer's Book*

of Days. Tucson: The University of Arizona Press, 2001.

"PROMISCUOUS 10% 'FUEL SEX CRISIS.'" *BBC News.* 14 Oct. 2004

<http://news.bbc.co.uk/1/hi/health/3741884.stm>
"PROSTITUTES' RIGHTS DEMONSTRATION IN SOUTH ASIA." *Prostitution Issues.* 15 Oct. 2004
<http://www.bayswan.org/seasian.html>

"PROSTITUTION IN THE UNITED STATES—THE STATISTICS." *Prostitutes Education Network.* 12 Dec. 2003
<http://www.bayswan.org/stats.html>

"RAPE OF WOMEN DURING WARTIME: BEFORE DURING, AND SINCE WORLD WAR II." *Religious Tolerance.* 10 Apr. 2004

<http://www.religioustolerance.org/war_rape.htm>

ROLHEISER, RON. "Effects of Sex Abuse on Children." *The-Tidings.* 25 Nov. 2004

<http://www.the-tidings.com/2003/0110/rolheiser_text.htm>

SCHMITT, ERIC. "Reports of Rape in pacific Spur Air Force Steps." *New York*

Times. 9 Mar. 2004
<http://www.nytimes.com/2004/03/09/politics/09MILI.html?hp>

SCIOLINO, ELAINE. "In France, Boys 'Take Turns' at Gang Rape." *Arizona Daily Star* 25 Oct. 2003: A18.

"SCIENCE OF THE SEXES: 2. DIFFERENT BY DESIGN.*" The Discovery Channel*. DVD: 2003.

SHLAIN, LEONARD. *Sex, Time and Power: How Women's Sexuality Shaped Human*

Evolution. New York: Viking, 2003.

SINGH, GAUTAM. "Acid Attacks Take Brutal Toil in India." *Arizona Daily Star*. 30 May 2004: A23.

"SINGLE-SEX EDUCATION." *National Association for Single Sex Public Education.*

27 Aug. 2004 http://www.singlesexschool.org/

"SINGLE-SEX VS. COED: THE EVIDENCE." *National Association for Single Sex Public Education*. 31 Aug. 2004 http://www.singlesexschool.org/research-singlesexvscoed.htm>

"SISTERS GIVE BIRTH AT 12, 14, 16." *BBC News*. 23 May 2005 <http://

news.bbc.co.uk/1/hi/uk/4572219.stm>

SMITH, ALEXANDER MCCALL. *Morality for Beautiful Girls*. New York: Random, 2001.

STANTON, GLENN T. "Fact Sheet on Divorce in America." *Smart Marriages.* 16 Dec. 2004

<http://www.smartmarriages.com/divorce_brief.html>

"STATISTICS: WORLDWIDE." *amfAR.* July 2012. 26 July 2012 <http://www.smfar.org/About_HIV_and AIDS/Facts_and_Stats/Statistics>

STOLL, CLIFFORD. "Internet Pioneer Reverses Course, Calling Computers Mostly a

Waste." Interview by Aline McKenzie. *The Dallas Morning News* 4 Aug.1998: 2F.

STUHLDREHER, KAREN. "State Rape: Representations of Rape in Viet Nam." *Nobody Gets off the Bus: The Viet Nam Generation Big Book.* 21 Apr. 2004

<http://lists.village.Virginia.edu/sixties/HTML_docs/Texts/Schol arly/
Stuhldreher_Rape.html>

SWALES, MICHAELA. "Pain and Deliberate Self-Harm." *The Welcome Trust.*2 June 2005
<http://www.wellcome.co.uk/en/pain/microsite/culture4.html>

"TAKING THE BULLY BY THE HORNS." 23 Apr. 2005
<http://www.tnmediators.com/bullies/statistics.htm>

"TEXTS AIM TO FIGHT AIDS IN KENYA." *BBC News.* 1 Dec. 2004

<http://news.bbc.co.uk/1/hi/technology/4054475.stm>

"THIS IS WHAT HAPPENS TO THE CHILDREN." *SOHOPEFUL International.* 2 June 2005<http://www.sohopeful.org/intl/facts/2004/fatherless_homes .html>

"TRAUMA IN THE LIVES OF THOSE WHO SELF-HARM."
Fragmented Mind. 18 Nov. 2004
<http://www.fragmentedmind.healthyplace2.com/custom2.html>

"TV 'INCREASES CHILD OBESITY RISK." *BBC News*. 20 May 2005

<http://news.bbc.co.uk/1/hi/health/4562879.stm>

"TV TIME LINKED TO TENDENCY TO BE A BULLY."
Arizona Daily Star 10 Apr. 2005: A3.

"U.N. WOMEN'S RIGHTS CRUCIAL TO AIDS FIGHT." *The New York Times*. 14 Nov.

2004
<http://www.nytimes.com/aponline/international/AP_Worldwide-AIDS.html>

"UNIVERSAL DECLARATION OF HUMAN RIGHTS." *BBC World Service.* 22 Dec.
2003<http://www.bbc.co.uk/worldservice/people/features/haveari
ghtto/four_b/full_text.shtml>

"U. S. TEENAGE PREGNANCY STATISTICS WITH COMPARATIVE STATISTICS FOR WOMEN

AGED 20-24." *The Alan Guttmacher Institute.* 2 June 2005
<http://

www.guttmacher.org/pubs/teen_stats.html>

VERRENGIA, JOSEPH B. "Modern American Family: Always in Motion, Child-

Dominated, Strained and Losing Intimacy." *Arizona Daily Star* 20 Mar. 2005: A14.

WAGNER, MARSDEN. "Midwifery in the Industrialized World." *Society of*

Obstetricians and Gynaecologists of Canada Nov. 1998. 1 May 2005

<http://www.msystems.net/family/Midwifery_Industrialized-World.html>

---. "Technology in Birth: First Do No Harm." *Midwifery Today.* 1 May 2005

<http://www.midwiferytoday.com/articles/technologyinbirth.asp>

WEST, ANDREW. "The Boys Who Will Be Gentlemen." 31 Aug. 2004

<http://www.smh.com.au/articles/2003/07/05/1057179204769.html?oneclick=true>

WHITEHOUSE, ANNA. "Managing Elephants: Lessons from Behavioural Studies."

26 Dec. 2003 <http://z00.upe.ac.za/teru/Elephants/Contents.pdf>

WINTERS, REBECCA. "A New Marriage Proposal." *Time* 8 Nov. 2004: 58-60.

World Sex Guide. Germany. 15 Oct.2004<http://www.worldsexguide.org/germany.html>

---. Netherlands. 15 Oct. 2004 < http://www.worldsexguide.org/netherlands.html>

WRIGHT, ROBERT. "Up from Gorilla Land: The Hidden Logic of Love and Lust."

Psychology Today. Mar/Apr.1995. 10 July 2003 <http://www.psychologytoday.com/htdocs/prod/ptoarticle/pto-19950301-000023.asp>

X, ALAN, with Amy Hammel-Zabin. "The Mind of a Child Molester." *Psychology*

Today. July/Aug. 2003: 67-71.

ZAVIS, ALEXANDRA. "Rape, Anarchy Rampant Throughout Liberia."

Arizona Daily Star 10 Aug. 2003: A19.

###

The THINGS WE DO